My Bucket List Has A Hole In It

L.E. HEWITT

SEABOARD PRESS

JAMES A. ROCK & COMPANY, PUBLISHERS

My Bucket List Has A Hole In It by L. E. Hewitt

SEABOARD PRESS

is an imprint of JAMES A. ROCK & CO., PUBLISHERS

My Bucket List Has A Hole In It copyright ©2015 by L.E. Hewitt

Special contents of this edition copyright ©2015 by Seaboard Press

Address comments and inquiries to:
SEABOARD PRESS
1937 West Palmetto Street, #6
Florence, South Carolina 29501

E-mail:
jrock@rockpublishing.com   lrock@rockpublishing.com
Internet URL: www.rockpublishing.com

Trade Paperback ISBN: 978-1-59663-876-1

Printed in the United States of America

First Edition: 2015

*Interested readers may
wish to visit the author's website:*

www.lehewitt.net

Dedicated to
Laura, Sara and Eric

Contents

Foreword

You have to take charge of your life instead of letting it take charge of you. I say that often to people I care about when they are struggling. I say this because we often take time for granted and time is the one thing you cannot buy, beg or borrow to gain more. I am just like anybody else. I have had my own struggles. A stroke, a divorce, kids growing up and moving on with their own lives, these are just a part of living. But there is no reason now to find something to smile about, something to be thankful about every single day. Just go out there and make it happen. Do what is in your heart.

You will make mistakes. I have made some whoppers in my life so far and will certainly make many more. When you do end up in that position, admit your wrongs and move forward. Also, forgive those who may have wronged you. Quite often this was not their intention and remember, they are just human too. Don't dwell on these negative moments, but instead take time to cherish the love and the laughter along the way. Those are the things worth your attention.

Personally, I go through life looking for the funny things or the good and happy things that happen every single day around me. That is the well from which I draw my stories. In almost every situation, you can find a positive. In almost every moment, you can choose how to react. Kindness and forgiveness can go a long way toward a better world.

I have gone through many drastic changes over the past few years. Many of them, both good and bad, I could never have predicted. The cool thing is that your dreams can change. Your goals can change. It is up to you to make those changes good. You may lose the chance to experience certain things along the way, but you may also find even better things down the road. So, "My Bucket List Has Got a Hole In It," but that doesn't mean that my life has stopped being an amazing place to reside.

Mormon Girls Rock

I have been on the road a lot. I have been up and down the highway frequently. I enjoy being out and about in some ways. I like observing the scenery and the people I encounter. This recent round of travels has led me to a major decision. I want to be a Mormon.

There are a whole bunch of billboards out along the highways these days with pictures of various people on them and the slogan "I am Mormon". I don't run across many Mormons in Indiana, but I can tell you from these billboards that the Mormon women are all beautiful! There is not a homely face amongst them! I am so impressed! Most churches I have ever gone to are mostly filled with blue-haired ladies wearing funny hats. It is refreshing to see no such women amongst this Mormon crowd.

I will have a lot of catching up to do on church doctrine. From what little I know, I think that they believe similar to other Christians except they say that Jesus reappeared in America some years back with additional instructions. I have no problem with their pronouncements, as I am neither qualified to prove nor disprove their assertions. All I know is that according to these billboards I keep seeing, Mormon girls rock!

FuzzButt Reports

Greetings, friends! FuzzButt here. Please do not tell my goofy owner that I can type. I normally would not disclose such a human talent, however I feel the need to set the record straight on a few things around here. I know that my "owner," and I use that term loosely, has been writing things from time to time about my behaviors. Now I believe it is time for you to hear the other side of the story.

For beginners, I only permit him to serve me. Where he gets this idea that he is the boss is beyond reasoning. Do I go out and find food for him while he lies in a patch of sun coming through the window sleeping on a cold winter's day? Do I clean his toilet? Is he the one who gets to hide behind the chair and scare the crap out of the dog when it walks by? I think not!

My poor "owner" is a nutcase. He fills his milk bowl with some kind of stuff that looks like haybales. He takes perfectly smelly fish and covers it up with crushed almonds and then cooks it! Don't get me wrong. Fish is great whether you heat it up or not. But throw that almond crap in the trash! I hate having to pick around all of that stuff every time I steal a meal from the counter.

And why does he get mad when I drink from his water glass? The dog doesn't seem to mind when I drink from its bowl? Besides, I do let the "owner" pet me and rub my belly sometimes when it is convenient for me. I even allow him to feel good by then treating me with some of that turkey he keeps in the refrigerator drawer.

I think I hear him using the can opener! I need to go for now but will try to write more again another time!

My Wardrobe

Some people think that I have too many clothes. I think they are nuts. I don't run to the mall all of the time or change fashions with the new season. I am a simple man. I have my lounging around clothes … jeans, sweats, t-shirts and such. I have my dressy clothes … slacks, button down shirts, ties. I also have dress casual clothes … khakis, pullovers, etc. … Sounds fairly normal to me! Don't you think?

Oh, and I do have a few other odd and end pieces. I have some old clothes with stains or rips that I use when working around the house. That is certainly practical, right? And I have my 7th grade physical education shirt, and the slick, silky orange striped dress shirt I used to wear when I went disco dancing in the 1970's. I also have the platform dress shoes I wore with it. This shows my intelligence. I know that fashions eventually come back around and I will be ready! I have a t-shirt from a band I was in from about 1980. All I need to do is shed half my body weight and I can still wear it. And there is that colonial outfit I wore in a parade in 1976. What's wrong with that? And that one pair of jeans I really liked when my waist was 4 inches smaller. Hey, you never know! I have a pair of insulated coveralls and boots in case I need to do any wintertime farming here in the suburbs. One needs to be prepared. A rogue herd of cattle may escape and run rampant through my neighborhood. I will be the only guy who is ready. I have a black trench coat, a winter coat, a denim jacket, a couple of hoodies, and a Mister Rogers grey sweater. I am a man of many graces, what can I say? Every stitch of clothing I own is a necessity. Now, if only I could find two socks that match …

Negativity

It often seems to me that dogs and cats often treat one another in a more civilized manner than people do. Why are humans so mean? This was on my mind today during a telephone call I made to someone I don't even know. This woman was mad at me from the moment she picked up the phone. She did not know who I was or why I was calling, but she was determined to let me have it! Why would she choose to behave like that? She has never seen me or talked to me before, yet you would swear she hated my guts. People are just funny like that sometimes. I bet if I had told her I was calling because she had just won the Publisher's Clearing House sweepstakes she would have turned all nice and sweet in an instant. But which would have been real? The mean old biddy or her sweet-as-pie alter ego?

I do not take it personally when someone is mean like that. I feel sorry for them. What a waste of good energy. If they only realized how silly it makes them appear. Have I ever been mean to someone? Absolutely. Did I look silly? I bet I did. Everybody makes mistakes. It is just that some people seem to conduct their whole lives in the negative.

Getting Organized

Its been a busy, but good week. I got a lot accomplished, I didn't have any major headaches with which to contend. All in all, things went well. Now comes the weekend. It's supposed to be sunny and warm! I am looking forward to laying in my hammock on the patio while the maid cleans the house and the chef cooks me up a special treat to snack upon. Boy, if only! Maybe I could find somebody to volunteer to be my maid, chef and butler for the weekend. Someone to lay out my clean clothes, bring me my breakfast and the newspaper, clean up my messes. Maybe they could clean up out in the yard too and organize the Mancave. That's not too much to ask, is it? Besides, I am a busy man and one look at me and it is easy to see that I could use my beauty rest. But no, there is no rest for me! I will be tinkering on stuff all weekend because there are like a million things that need done around here right now! That one door latch is not working right and the driveway cement has gotten some cracks and that one tree over in the side yard needs hauled away and cut up and the railing going down the steps is loose again and the cabinet in the corner of the kitchen has a loose hinge and the car needs cleaned out again and the … boy! Just thinking about all of this stuff has exhausted me! I should probably go lay down and ponder on a plan of action before I get started. It's good to be organized you know!

Another Saturday

It's Saturday night, about 7:15pm. In my youth and twenties, this would have meant I was getting ready to go to work. I played music almost every Saturday night from 10pm until 2am somewhere. My day would have started about 9am and I would not get back to bed until around 4am Sunday. I would be tired, but not exhausted.

What's different now? Well, let's see. A typical Saturday I will be up about 8:30am, so not much different there. I don't play music in public anymore. I have considered it, but never followed through on the idea. My bedtime now? Oh, about 9:30pm … and I am pooped!

Where has all of that youthful energy gone? Where is that ambition to spend endless days experiencing stuff? Why does a nap in the afternoon now sound better than just about any other activity I can think of?

Don't get me wrong. I am a busy active guy. I am involved in many things. But now when my batteries run dry, I am ready to hit the sack! I used to laugh at my mom for always falling asleep when we would watch a movie on television. Now my kids make fun of me for the same thing. One day I even fell asleep at the movie theater! I have to admit it was a good place to nap.

I still frequently act like a kid and I play games and stay active. I just seem to pay for it more at the end of the day now.

So here I am. Another exciting Saturday night! I might make me some Ovaltine and watch Star Trek. Or I think there may be another NCIS marathon on tonight! Livin' on the edge, baby!

Sing a Positive Tune

I have been thinking about all of the things that we just accept in life. The things that we just assume are the best way to do things. Most of us assume that we are supposed to eat three meals a day and that certain foods are just meant for eating at a certain time of day. Why?

We also believe that our yards should be covered by grass and mowed to a certain uniform look. We assume that our cars should have four wheels … why? Would a six wheeled car not work as well? I have no idea. I am just curious.

We believe that a CEO should make more than a garbage man. Why? Who has the harder job?

We believe that we should do or act in certain ways because "I was raised that way". Really?

I would bet that people 500 years ago felt the same way. Think of how different our lives are today than theirs were.

Now take that same thought 500 years into the future. Will they also look at us as primitive? Probably.

Will their lives in turn be simplistic compared to those who come after them? I bet so.

So are our ways of doing things "modern"? Probably not in the bigger picture. There will probably be better ways to do just about every activity of daily life.

But, we do not live in the past or the future. We live in the present. We need to embrace and treasure all that our lives have to offer while not thinking of ourselves as any better or worse than those that came before us or those who are yet to come.

Each and every one of us just sort of "arrived" here one day. We had no choice whether we were rich or poor or boy or girl or white or black or short or tall or ugly or pretty … on the outside. We do however control what is inside. The things we should focus on are how much love and kindness and forgiveness we can spread in one lifetime. Learn to treasure the moments and the experience of living with all other living things. Why waste the one life you get on hatred and disdain and conflict and anger. None of us are perfect, yet we are all works of perfection, amazing living beings.

Death of an Adversary

Someone I know died today. He had been given a very grim prognosis a couple of months ago. What make this death odd for me is that he and I did not get along. We had a disagreement over an issue a few years ago. I thought he was in the wrong and I am sure he felt the same way about me. We still encountered one another on a regular basis, but we simply ignored one another or avoided communication. We coexisted peacefully but never resolved our differences. He was not a bad guy and he probably would have said the same about me. We just viewed the world differently and in the end I think that we were both ok with that.

I was saddened to hear of his untimely passing and I hope he has found his peaceful eternity. I also hope that his family finds comfort in his unwavering religious faith.

I wish conflicts around the world were more like the one that defined our relationship. People will not always agree, but they should still be able to live side by side in peace. What real good ever comes from endless conflict. Simply realize you are different and move on. In the end, proving that you are "right" only proves to make you wrong.

Wait For Me

I attended a seminar this week. It was a 7 hour class on a very dry and boring subject. We could have covered all of the necessary materials in 5 hours if not for her. You know the one. Sometimes it is a man and sometimes a woman, but there is always that one person who sits in the front on the right side who just is obsessed with asking stupid questions. The type of questions where even the instructor starts rolling their eyes. The thing that I cannot understand is why there is always one of them. Never zero, never ten, always one. Is there some committee somewhere who makes sure that one of these whatever you want to call them attends every meeting known to man? Do these people not realize that every other person in the room is contemplating what sort of sentence they might get for silencing them and debating if it would indeed be worth it? A question every now and then from various members of the audience is fine, but when one person asks more than the whole combined, there's a problem. I was a good boy and remained polite all day. I stayed out of trouble. I did, however, snap a picture of her with my phone so I can take it to Kinko's this weekend so that I can have it blown up into a poster for me to throw rocks at. Maybe I should get one made of that guy down the street who was out mowing his grass this week too. It's mid-March for Heaven's sake! Go back inside and watch basketball or something! Then when you see me pull out my mower in mid-May, you will know it is time.

Where's My Underwear?

There are a lot of problems in this world. Many things to worry about. Global warming, nuclear proliferation, who is stealing my underwear … what? Yes, nuclear proliferation belongs on my list. It is a big deal! Oh, my underwear? That may be the biggest mystery of all.

I keep buying new packages of four of a certain brand of underwear. I am the only person in this house who wears that size or type or color. After the laundry is done I usually have one of the four pairs left. What's up with that? Eventually, even that one pair will disappear as well. I have bought twelve pairs of new underwear in the past three months. Where have they gone? Somebody has a crapload of new boxer briefs in their house, but it ain't me.

I have developed a list of suspects. Maybe its a manager from the store where I buy them. Is he stealing them back so that I will spend more money? There is always Fuzzbutt. He steals ponytail holders and socks and pork chops, so why not underwear. Of course it could be one of my millions of adoring fans … one of the more obsessed ones I would think. Maybe its the lady at the bank. She has shifty eyes. It could be my mother. She always said to be sure I had on clean underwear "just in case". Maybe she is checking up on me.

I just know that I am tired of spending all of my money on something such as … wait! I just saw Fuzzbutt racing by with something big with red and white stripes in his mouth! Could it be? If so, I will soon be advertising for a new owner for him!

I'm Not Old

Recently I was in a group of people who were talking about age when one gentleman said, "You're in your fifties, right?" How dare him! How could he possibly think that I am anywhere near fifty! I was so hurt! Then, a few days later there was this elderly woman who said I looked just like some preacher she watches on TV! She could not recall his name, but she left me wondering what devilishly handsome man she could be talking about.

To make matters worse, there have been two different observations about my laugh recently. One person keeps saying I laugh like Santa Claus and another says I laugh like the pigs on Angry Birds!

The Suspicious Box

Fuzzbutt is stalking a box. He knows it wasn't there yesterday and surely there must be something evil and sinister inside! Elizabeth is lying on the living room floor playing on her computer. She is probably getting caught up on her whole social world. Me? I am getting ready to get ready. What I mean is that I am getting ready to get dressed. In other words, I am being lazy.

I have no right to be lazy. My ancient ancestors were not lazy. They didn't have that luxury. They had to find food and fresh water every day. And they had to avoid being eaten by some other hungry critter. As for me, if I get hungry I go to the refrigerator. If I get too hot or cold, I push a little button on the wall. All of these luxuries I owe to those who were curious and industrious and figured out how to make our lives so easy. I am very lucky to be living at this point in time.

Speaking of time, there is never enough of it. Time is the most valuable thing in the universe. Each of us is only given a small bit of it. How we use it is up to us. The way we use time often changes as we progress through life. Our priorities change. These days I am trying to stop and enjoy the moments as often as possible. I take great pleasure from these little moments. For instance, as I have been writing this, Fuzzbutt has been continuing his assault on the box. I have been highly entertained by this. He would circle around and then move in a bit closer then circle more, stopping to sniff the air from time to time checking for the scent of danger. He finally made it up to the edge of the box and peeked in. Upon finding the box vacant, he decided it was a good place to settle down for a nap.

As my luck would have it, shortly thereafter Smoky entered the room and noticed the same foreign box. He too began his own tactical assault upon it. When he reached the edge of the box and peered in, he scared the crap out of both himself and Fuzzbutt.

Poor Frank

I had a strange voicemail yesterday. First of all, it was Memorial Day. Secondly, it was somebody who sounded really mad. They said, "I just wanted you to know that I am suing you. What you did was wrong. You will be hearing from my lawyer soon." Unfortunately, they called me Frank. If they are suing me, they should at least get my name right. Poor Frank, whoever he is. Trouble is a comin'. But then I got to thinking. If this caller had really hired a lawyer and was suing Frank, why would he call and threaten him? Wouldn't that just jeopardize his case? I bet he was just trying to scare poor old Frank straight. Frank probably thinks they are still buddies. I wonder what it was that Frank did to cause all of this. The truth be known, it is probably something not even worth fighting about. Anyhow, if your name is Frank, you probably should watch your back for a few days. Somebody is out to get you and they are toting a lawyer.

All Gone

It is soooo frustrating. I am soooo distressed. I have been having a craving for chocolate milk and somebody has stolen my Ovaltine! I have looked in all of the cabinets and closets in the kitchen and it is nowhere to be found. Somebody is gonna pay! I am not in the mood for white milk. I want chocolate! Who could be so mean as to do such a thing? My needs are quite simple in life. For someone to steal this simple pleasure from me is simply inexplicable.

These kids think that everything that enters this house is fair game! Do they not realize that, as the man, I get certain rights? They steal my pillows and my socks, my graham crackers and my car keys, my TV remote and my spare change. Why is it I never catch them using the lawnmower without permission, or weeding the flowerbeds? I have never once caught them doing my laundry or changing the oil in the car. They are sneaky stealing heathens, I tell you!

Ribfest

Wow, what a week! Busy, busy, busy. I have gotten a lot accomplished. I have had long, good days. I made much progress on some things I had been working on. But, best of all, I had five free meals in nice restaurants! I am gonna be fat ... Ummm, maybe I should say I already am!

One of the free meals was baked salmon. That one was healthy for me. Salmon, grilled potatoes, asparagus and carrots. That was me being a good boy! I did taste a gyro as well that someone else was eating. I only ate about half of their meal.

Then there was the buffet. It was at a place that has just about everything. I ate chicken and crab and fish and steak and potatoes and salad and pudding and watermelon. That is at least what I can remember. The guy beside me had crawfish and octopus. I did not eat half of his meal.

The next freebie was Mexican. A chimichanga as big as my head with chips, salsa, beans and rice.

Then came the Ribfest. It was a competition between chefs to see who could make the best BBQ ribs. I was invited to come and pass my judgment, so I tried them all so that I could be fair in my voting, of course! The one that won my vote did not have the best sauce on it. I chose it because it was sooo tender. It was a hard job. I told them I would be happy to come back again next time just so nobody else has to be exposed to the stress of making that decision.

Trading Cars

I decided that I was tired of the kids making fun of my old car, so I went out this week and bought a newer one. On his first trip with me, Will had several comments. He was quick to note that something was drastically wrong. All of the windows rolled up and down properly. There was a lack of lighted red lights on the dash console. There was this really cold air blowing from the vents. The back seats were not full of my files. I guess I should have expected the ribbing.

The amazing part for me came later. You see, I did not get rid of my old car. I just added to the fleet. So I figured I could still drive my old friend around from time to time. However, those same sweet children who made fun of my car for so many years are now fighting over which one will now inherit it. Yep, Will and Elizabeth are both laying claim to it. I guess all those red dashboard lights are not so uncool after all!

Not Feeling Sorry

It has been hot. Over 100 degrees at times. I have been running from air conditioned car to air conditioned house all week. I feel sorry for those who do not have that luxury.

I do not feel sorry for the guy I saw jogging about one o'clock Thursday afternoon when the thermometer said it was 98 outside, or for the dummy I saw mowing her grass that same afternoon. We haven't even had any rain to speak of in a month! And I cannot say it is because of her watering program either, because her grass was as brown as mine! I also do not feel sorry for the woman I saw walking on Friday in 100 degree heat wearing all black long pants and long sleeved shirt. Me? I would run around naked when it is this hot if I could get away with it.

Summers Long Ago

I am so busy these days. I always have stuff to do. I left the house this morning at 8:00am and did not get back home tonight until nearly 10:00pm. Am I that important? No way! I am nothing special. I am just some hillbilly from Pennsylvania. I ate two fancy meals while I was out today and never paid a dime. I spent an hour addressing a room of ladies who acted like I had something important to say. If they only knew that I am really no smarter than their dog. I just smell better ... usually. If they only knew that I would be just as happy having stick races down a creek or playing football in the mud or making ice cream by taking my turn cranking the handle. I would be just fine with that. The trouble is that it doesn't pay very well. Well actually the ice cream cranking pays better. Nothing can compete with a bowl of freshly made vanilla!

It has been a hot summer. Good ice cream weather. The trouble is that I live in an air conditioned world. You think that's a good thing? I will admit that its great when it comes time to sleep, but the air conditioner has taken some good things from me as well. There is something relaxing about laying in front of a fan as it blows across your head. Also, air-conditioning has nearly eliminated porch sitting. Growing up, we spent most summer evenings on the porch staying cool in the shade. We did not just sit there, either. Usually there were beans to shell or corn to husk or vegetables to cut and clean. I would always swing on the poles on my back porch for entertainment too. They were the poles that held the roof up. I would swing on them until mom yelled at me to stop. I never seemed to get her properly trained about how those poles were really there just for every kid who ever showed up at our place to swing on and that holding up the roof was just a secondary function.

I would trade those summer days for the ones I have now in a heartbeat.

Cat Toys

I recently bought a new laser pointer, the kind that makes a little red dot on anything you point it toward. I buy one from time to time because they make such a good cat toy. We have four cats running around here. They need some entertainment. It is funny how they all treat this little red dot differently.

Blackie plays it cool. She waits until the dot's almost upon her and then she pounces. She typically tries to remain quite graceful and proper. Smoky, on the other hand, will make a mad dash clear across the room and then chase the dot in circles until he is so dizzy he can't stand up. He will then take thirty seconds to recompose himself before starting right into the same thing again. I never claimed he was the smartest of the bunch. Goldie is about fourteen years old and overweight. She LOVES the red dot. She will chase it all over the place until she needs to stop and have an asthma attack. She will then stop, cough a bit, clean her paws and her butt, then resume the red dot attack. I am not sure what the cleaning has to do with anything, but she always does it.

Then there is Fuzzbutt. He simply sits there and stares with amazement at the stupidity of the other three for chasing a little red dot! He pays no attention at all to the laser. For whatever reason, he sees this game as pointless since there is obviously no real food involved. He appears to think he is smarter than the rest of them. Doesn't anybody realize that ponytail holders are way more fun? Yep, he can be found almost daily with a stolen ponytail holder playing joyfully under the dining room table.

Good Intentions

I just got home from a long bike ride. I feel great, tired but great. I am more active than most people my age. I have also been playing racquetball more recently too. Talk about a good workout! On top of this, I have been eating very healthy and trying not to overeat. That's right, my life is no fun right now! Actually, I have no complaints. I feel good and I get handsomer every day.

The older I get, the more difficult it is to stay fit. It is so easy to just become lazy. So easy to just eat all the bad stuff. The problem is that the less you do, the less you want to do. The less energy you have. Conversely, the more you do, the better you feel, and you actually have more energy too. That has never really made sense to me. So I try to do a lot these days. And overall life is darned good.

I do wish the lady at the bank would contact me. I could use an extra million or two. And I wish I saw more of my children. They are busy doing their own things these days. But otherwise, things are good. My health is good, my stress is low and I am smiling a lot.

I don't always do the right things or make the best decisions, but my heart is in the right place. I mean well. Things don't always turn out that way, but it's not for lack of good intentions. We all make mistakes. We are human. It is what we do to move forward and correct those mistakes that makes us better people.

So when I sneak out to the kitchen in the middle of the night tonight for that big box of powdered doughnuts, I will be making a mistake, but my intentions will be good. I will be doing it because I would not want them to spoil. That would be a waste of food and my mom always told me not to waste food because there were people starving in other countries. So see I will just be trying to do good.

Tomorrow May Never Come

Every one of us makes mistakes. Every one of us has regrets. Every one of us has things we wish we could do over again. But, should one event or one short period define the entire rest of our lives? Or should we be more forgiving and understanding? Should we each remain angry and at odds? Or should we look at the entirety of our life and look to mend broken fences? Life is short. Love is scarce. And I do not intend to let one disagreement define the next forty years.

The things that we are missing are too great. Family, friends, shared moments. Those are too important to be thrown away. I miss the simple things. Throwing Frisbee in the front yard, my very own batch of bread pudding made with love, feeling that swell of pride at the end of a marathon. Those are big. Just think of the even bigger things to come in the future. Let's not miss out.

If you are reading this and do not understand it, that's ok. It is an open letter to one of the most important people in the world to me. What I hope you will do is apply this to your own life. Is there someone you should reach out to? Do it now, don't wait. Tomorrow could be too late.

Health Food

I am so happy! I found wild rice sticks at the store today! Also, I got some low fat cottage cheese and Granny Smith applesauce while I was there to eat for dinner! I am on a roll!

Actually, I am off the rolls, and the butter, and the meatloaf, and the mac-n-cheese, just to name a few. I am on a healthy food and weight loss kick. Let's go back a few years. Seventeen years ago I quit smoking. I weighed probably 145 lbs. I am right at 6 ft tall. I was SKINNY! I could not gain weight if I tried. When I quit smoking, I replaced it with eating. I mean I really ate big for six months. As an example, I could polish off 2 footlongs at Subway no problem! It was better than the cigarettes. At the end of the six months my cravings had subsided, my eating slowed and I weighed 185 lbs. That was fine for someone my height. From there I slowly gained over the years until, in 2002, I got on the scale and was horrified to see that I had broken the 200 lb barrier. I went on a healthy eating/exercising binge and lost 38 lbs, down to a lean, mean 165 lbs. I looked and felt great. Life moved on and slowly I let old, bad habits creep back into my diet. I ended up setting a new personal record at 213 lbs. I got mad! I am too pretty to be fat! At least that's what I told myself. The truth is that I am just an old ugly fart, but I want to be a skinny, healthy, old ugly fart.

The first time, ten years ago, the weight just melted off of me. I lost a pound almost every day. This time, probably due to age, it is much harder. Matter of fact, I started this last year and then started to get lazy, but this time I am determined to win! I am reclaiming my body! The key is that I am making it fun. I am riding my bicycle several miles most evenings. I am also playing racquetball for two hours at a time. These things keep my heart pumping. I am eating small meals several times a day consisting of natural things and I have lost eight pounds in the past three weeks. It would be so easy to just let myself go and be fat. I could hit 250lbs in no time. But I know how much better and more energetic I feel when I am fit and skinny.

Healthy food is hard! I could run in the kitchen right now and grab a can of soda and a handful of chips, so easy! Or I could slice up a cucumber, which I also like, but that requires work. I am tired. I had a long day. Don't you feel sorry for me? I need a personal chef. That's where it gets difficult. Healthy foods often require work. If McDonalds made you go in the kitchen and grind your own hamburger and cut your own potatoes for the fries, then you would be less likely to crave a Big Mac. And why does my body crave stuff that is bad for me anyhow? I have never heard someone complain that they were gonna just die if they didn't get to eat a raw carrot soon! Or "I need my All Bran in the morning or I just can't function". Never once has someone said to me, "I recently had to cut down to just three rice cakes a day." People can go to a party and brag about having six beers. Do you ever hear them mention drinking six bottles of water in an afternoon? Or " I am sorry man, I ate your last orange. I just couldn't help myself!"

Well, those times are changing for me baby! I am running into the kitchen right now and stuffing myself on bottled water and wild rice sticks! Be jealous!

Beach Volleyball

I am scheduled to play beach volleyball today at 2:30 … in Louisville, Kentucky. Now in case you are wondering which ocean that is on, let me help you … none! I am being summoned to a beach with no water for this event. It must be like those people on the Olympics who play on a court of sand surrounded by spectators. I am sure I will have fun and make a fool of myself. I won't even be the oldest fart out there running around. One fella is in his seventies and in better shape than anybody. He is amazing. He ran the local half marathon in May, yes that's 13.1 miles, and he regularly plays soccer and racquetball and he is good! He can beat most men half his age! I am inspired by people like that. I will be turning fifty in a few months and I am proud of my physical condition. I know it is better than many, but to know there is also hope in my seventies is awesome.

I do have a fashion dilemma though. I know many of the beach volleyball players on tv wear those tight fitting Speedo trunks. So, I went to that big sporting goods store over at the mall to get me a pair. When I asked the young woman working there where I could find Speedos for men my age, she looked at me like I was nuts.

Obviously, she is not a beach volleyball player. So then I said, "You know! Those tight fitting trunks you see guys on TV wearing. Can you help me pick out a pair that looks good on me?"

She looked me up and down and replied with disdain, "No, that's not possible."

I am not sure what her problem was. I guess she was just too busy with other tasks to help me.

Olympian

The Olympics are in full swing. Swimming, running, gymnastics, boxing and basketball. Some of these people are amazing. Equestrian ... wait a minute ... doesn't the horse do the most of the work there? Does the horse get to keep the medal in the barn? Air pistol ... what? Air pistol? What kind of sport is that? Mom never considered me an athlete when I had my BB gun. She considered me a threat to society. And what are those things that look like headphones on the water polo teams swim caps? Where do you go to play water polo anyhow? I have never ever seen it live in my life.

Now table tennis. There is a sport! I was an awesome table tennis player in my babysitter's basement. I may have been the town champion ... all 200 of us. I should have probably pursued my Olympic table tennis dreams. I was too pretty for boxing. I cant jump very high. I can run fairly fast if something mean is chasing me.

Maybe its not too late. My old BB gun may be in mom's garage. I need to get started training. I only have four years to get ready. I can practice shooting the kids in the butt.

Physically Speaking

I am having a rough week physically. Some people claim that it is because I need to stop acting like I am a kid. I refuse to buy that. Heck, I am only 49! But, back to my week. The trouble started last Friday. I was in Louisville playing beach volleyball. Yes, I know, there are no beaches in Louisville, but they do have a place with a bunch of sand and volleyball nets surrounded by a snack bar and tables and bleachers. The games were fun. Well, at least until this one big gorilla hit me square in the nose with an elbow as I dove for the ball! Nearly one week later my nose bone is still sore!

I know by now you are already feeling sorry for me. But wait, it gets worse! Yesterday evening I was invited to play racquetball with my friend. He has been enjoying beating me in recent matches. Well, last night I was doing well at extracting my revenge. Until about the middle of our fourth game that is! That is when he hit a ball to the back wall in such a way that it caused me to hit myself right between the eyes with my racquet, resulting in a one inch bleeding gash right between my eyebrows. It's all his fault! He is just jealous of my pretty face! He claims that since I hit myself I cannot blame him. I say he planned it! He was just out to get me! I know this because in the previous game he hit the ball squarely into my left boob! So tonight as I sit here, my nose hurts, my forehead hurts, and my bruised boob hurts!

Perfectly Normal

It's Friday night and I am ready for the weekend! I have been so busy all week. I have an exciting weekend planned! I am washing clothes and cleaning the house and then I get to mow the yard and maybe even clean out the car! My celebrity life is the envy of the world!

I have no complaints. I have a home. I even have air conditioning. I have food. I have good people in my life. I have pets. I have a car. I have good health. I have all that I need. I am lucky, very lucky.

There are many things that I want, but I do not need them to be happy. I want new floor mats for my car. I want to know next time before somebody gives me jellyfish to eat. I want my back to stop hurting. I want to get my fat belly flat again. I want some socks without holes in the toes. I want peaceful sleep.

The big thing is that I am just happy to be here. Happy for every day of life I have. I try to smile all day every day and mean it. Nothing is perfect, but my life is certainly close enough.

Weird People

I like weird people. Who the heck wants the world full of cookie cutter, generic, bland people? I like the unique ones with character who dance to their own beat … like the ones who can't dance to save their soul, yet they do it anyhow, with joy in their hearts. Who wants the world to be full of people who never take chances for fear of making a fool of themselves? I have one friend who can't carry a tune, yet they go to Karaoke places frequently, get up, and sing their heart out. Those who sit along the sidelines are missing out. So what if people look at you strange. They are just jealous because they are too insecure to take that same risk.

I try to make a fool of myself on a regular basis. I think it builds character. It is good to be humbled by my lack of abilities. For instance, I went back to the racquetball court last night for a rematch with my friend from Afghanistan. I went there with high hopes of redeeming myself since the last time when I cut my head open with my own racquet. I played well. I played hard. I was soaking wet with sweat. I lost five games and won zero! I think my friend needs to be deported. He is a professional racquetball player posing as an insurance agent. I just know it. I tried hitting it away from him, at him, behind him, in front of him, and over him. It didn't matter. He was like a fifty year old cheetah. I may have lost, but it sure was fun! And you know I will be out there trying again real soon.

Moments

Each life is made up of special moments, often unexpected, that leave a lasting impression. Those moments should be treasured forever. I can think of a few that will never leave me and always make me smile. Standing in the main lobby of the Opryland Hotel Playing my dad's acoustic guitar and singing "Silent Night" solo surrounded by a crowd of many hundreds on the main floor, and even more on the balcony level, was one of those moments for me. I did this same performance night after night and was very honored each and every time.

The Saturday night when I, as an eighteen year old, moved nervously across the floor at the local dinner club and asked the most beautiful girl I had ever seen to dance and she said yes. That was a moment never to be forgotten. I felt on top of the world.

Driving down an Indiana parkway when my cell phone rang and a woman on the line introduced herself and told me that her publishing company was interested in signing a contract to publish my first book.

Standing at the finish line of a 26.2 mile marathon running race and seeing my daughter, Shelly, round that final turn and head toward the finish, my heart was in my throat. I was filled with emotional pride for her massive accomplishment.

Those are some great ones. Some other memorable moments are not so great, but equally defining.

"Your dad passed away about 5 minutes ago."

"You have had a stroke."

"There is no other alternative than to euthanize her"

Those quotes are also burned into my memory.

Happy hellos and sad good-byes. Triumphs and failures. I am grateful for every single experience. Life is not always easy or always a big bowl of fun, but it is very much worth the journey.

The biggest thing I have learned is don't carry a grudge around forever. It's just not worth it. And never be afraid to tell others how you feel, especially if it is a positive. Make others smile and you will soon be smiling yourself.

Real Motivation

I get to go to a seminar tomorrow. I get to spend most of my day listening to some guy who is out to motivate me. He is supposed to make me feel all giddy inside, I guess. He is supposed to make me feel like I can conquer the world! Do you think he would object if I simply asked him to help me conquer my basement? The rest of the world can remain unconquered if I can just get ahead of the game in the basement.

There is one very large room and four smaller rooms down there and I need about an uninterrupted week down there to make sense of it all. Organizing and painting and new flooring and such. Maybe even a new wall to divide up the big room a bit. It is a beautiful space with a stone fireplace and bar area. It just has been neglected and has become a place for the kids to leave their junk. I just am not down there much these days. If I get it reorganized, then I may go down there to hang out sometimes.

This seminar guy would really motivate me if he just sent the whole group over here for the afternoon. We could knock out about half of my to do list downstairs. Maybe I will bring up the idea of a group field trip to him. Do you think he will go for it?

Expiration Dates

I have been pondering expiration dates. The milk in my fridge expires 8/28/2012, the eggs 9/1/2012, the canned corn in the cabinet 12/14/2013, the pain reliever in the medicine cabinet 3/1/2015. How the heck do they know that? What will occur inside that can of corn on December 13th of next year that will make it unfit to eat the next day? Will those eggs kill me on September 3rd? What makes all the eggs in that package go bad on the same day? What's the deal here?

The milk is a whole issue in itself. If I buy regular old milk, I typically will see that its expiration date is a couple of weeks away. However, if I buy the organic milk, the date may be a month and a half from now! What's the difference? It's still milk! How is that possible?

Then there is the honey! I recently read that there was honey discovered in ancient Egyptian tombs and it was still fresh! How did they know that? Was there a use by date printed on the side? How does honey stay fit to eat for thousands of years? Biscuits get stale by lunchtime!

I want to meet the person who figured all of this out. Is there a master chart out there? I want one! And I want to know exactly what I can expect to happen if I eat that corn for Christmas 2013.

Scratching My Head

Yesterday evening I went out to dinner with Elizabeth and a family friend. It was a kind of spur of the moment decision. They wanted me to go along to a sushi place with them. I struggle a bit with this cuisine, but I managed to find a good meal. I had a small salad with carrots, radishes, seaweed, and cucumbers in it. That was very good. I had some spider rolls made with soft shelled crab. Those were quite tasty as well and I was promised that no real spiders were used in the making of my spider rolls. For dessert, we three shared cookies and cream fried ice cream. Wow! Now that was something to write home about! A great ending to the meal.

After the meal they noticed that the big clothing store across the parking lot was having a moving sale. 30% off everything in the store. They felt they just had to go, so they dragged me along. While they shopped, I simply wandered around the store taking in the sights. I especially enjoy watching the people. I am forever fascinated by the endless mix of people in this world. However, it was one particular woman who stood out from the crowd.

This woman was a reasonably attractive, tall, slender woman who I would guess was in her late thirties or early forties. She was nicely dressed in black slacks and a top and had a gold band in her hair. She was wearing four inch platform heals and walking with a quad cane. What is wrong with this picture? This woman had no signs of a physical or mental handicap. She looked very fit and young. Yet, there was the cane. One of those silver ones with black rubber feet. Did she have the cane because she was a klutz? Was she living in fear of a shoe accident? Or did she have some sort of hidden injury? But if she had an injury, then why not wear flats? So many questions I had for this woman! And I will never know! It is still bugging me today!

L. E. for President

I have decided that I should run for President. I have looked at the competition and decided that I have a different viewpoint to contribute to the campaign. Here is what I intend to do when elected.

First, I will put forth a law that states that each member of Congress is forbidden to know how the others will vote on a piece of legislation ahead of time and must therefore base his or her vote on the merits of the bill and not upon party politics or re-election ramifications for his or her fellow party members.

Second, all members of Congress must relinquish all assets to the government, stay in office a maximum of eight years, and then leave to live on whatever is the median income for a family of four at the time his or her term ends. When these people will leave office as the middle class, I bet they will fight like the devil to make sure the middle class gets treated well. Any Congressman found attempting to hide assets under someone else's name will be required to resign immediately and live in a poor neighborhood on minimum wage.

I will sign a bill requiring the President to buy his own gas for Air Force One. This will drastically reduce campaign trips and vacations to places normal people cannot afford to go. Also, all elected officials will be limited to two weeks vacation per year and will be required to work most holidays. Public lie detector tests will be administered randomly to assure honesty.

If any military action is to be taken, the President and Congress must be in the first group of soldiers on the front lines. This should cut down on hostilities with other countries.

I will keep working on more items for my platform, but for now I simply ask for your vote.

Stories yet to Come

I like my home. I could live here all of the time if not for my busy schedule. I have lots of space, plenty of rooms, a Mancave, a big yard, and plenty of things to play with. What more could I want? I have a woodshop out in the garage, a music room downstairs, a big stone fireplace, a comfortable bed, and a big remote control. I even have food in the fridge! Now, all I need is a few million dollars and I will never need to leave.

My life is far from perfect, but it is still a very good life to have. I have kids and pets to keep me young. I have good friends and I get paid to tell my stories. Telling my stories is the easiest part. I can write about all of the fascinating stuff I find. All of the people I meet. I have a million stories yet to tell. Some of them I just need to wait on the person to die first to avoid any issues. For instance, the person that always claims somebody at their table is having a birthday every time they go out to eat just so they can snag free dessert. Or maybe the story about the deaf person who isn't and everybody knows it, yet for some reason they all just play along. Or the story of how one phone call once made me just sit right down in the middle of some stranger's house and after a minute I just got up and continued with no explanation. Or how does the term "pool mulch" have meaning to me? Or who once misunderstood a question I had asked and therefore proceeded to tell me about a bathroom in a bar in Tijuana. Or what is the sweetest sound I ever knew? Why was I chasing some strange dog in the dark at 3am? The complete story of the biggest lie ever perpetrated upon me. Only one other person in the whole world knows. Why am I partial to Denny's? Why do I like buckwheat cakes so much? How did my skateboard issue justice for me? Sweet revenge was that one!

I could go on and on. Life is so full of little moments. We often take these moments for granted. There is much to be learned and much entertainment value in just paying attention. I think I need to get busy on making more books!

Self Importance

I wish I knew why the heck I am here and what I am supposed to be doing. Am I here to learn some stuff? Am I here to accomplish something? Do I play some role in the grand scheme? Or am I just here?

It's a frustrating question, because there are no easy answers. We just have to accept that here we are and make the best of it. It is really something we have no control over. It's not like we have any other planets or galaxies available to us. It's not like we can simply will ourselves into being a tiger or a rabbit. We are just here. Either placed here by some intelligent being or else we just happen to exist in this moment out of pure luck or chance.

We all have the tendency to get self-important. We get to worrying about things that really don't matter.

We worry about the name on the clothes we wear or the kind of car we drive or whether we will make bail in time on Monday morning so as not to be late for work. We dwell on where to go for dinner or whether the neighbor keeps his grass mowed or how to act as if we don't notice while the dog we are walking on the leash poops in somebody else's driveway.

I get a kick out of neighborhood associations. They worry so much about what everybody is doing. Are they conforming to the standards set by a handful of people as to how we all should conduct our lives? Talk about silly stuff to worry about! They act as if nobody should know you own a garbage can or a satellite dish. Weirdos.

Driving Lessons

I really have it made these days. I don't have to get up at 5am to go to work or stay out until midnight just to earn a paycheck. I don't have to even leave the house if I don't want to. I get to be home to watch a football or hockey game on TV if I want, or I can go out to any event I choose without needing to worry about my schedule. My life is so easy now. It hasn't always been this way. I have worked two full time jobs at the same time. I have worked night shifts and varying shifts and sixteen hour shifts. I have done many different things along the way. I am just lucky. I have been able to find a way to pay the bills and still have control over my own time. I never take that blessing for granted.

Today is Saturday. I chose to work for a couple of hours, but then I took Will driving. He is getting ready to take his driver's test. We drove about twenty miles on a variety of roads, then we stopped at a store for me to pick up a new pair of my favorite reading glasses, then we stopped for ice cream. That was all for him. I did not have him stop at the ice cream shop for me. I did have to go ahead and eat some ice cream too, but that was just so he would not have to eat alone. I ate the ice cream solely to be a good dad. The sacrifices I make! After finishing the ice cream, Will drove us home. I also was able to take the time to set up a parallel parking obstacle course between the Jeep and the trash cans for him to practice. He did not hit the Jeep even once. I can't say the same for the trash cans.

—

Every day has its own unique moments. No two days are exactly the same. That is what makes life so fun. Take today, for instance. One of the memorable moments today took place in an office when a woman stated, "I am having a senior, blonde, menopausal moment." That struck fear in my heart and I quickly exited the premises.

Fried Pickle Euphoria

I have a confession to make. I cheated today. I know it was wrong. I know I was not thinking clearly. I know that no good can come of this. And I am here to confess my sins and move forward. I was driving on the southeast side of town down an old familiar street. That was when I felt that tug on my heart. I should not have stopped the car. I should not have gone inside. But oh how good it felt at the time. Yes, today I had fried pickles and a root beer float from that fifties diner across town. I cheated on my healthy diet I have been following. There! I said it! I have confessed my sins!

I have been eating very healthy and doing so good. I have been behaving. I really have! But today the urge was just too great. The root beer floats at that place are awesome, but I really think it was the fried pickles that got me. Those things are so hot and juicy and I just cannot stop myself until the bag is empty! I was in junk food heaven for about fifteen minutes, then the guilt set in. So now I am back to my carrots and celery and water. Take pity on my imperfect soul!

Grammy's Stew

Will was in the mood for a milkshake last night. He convinced me that he and I should go out to dinner to a place that has burgers and fries and shakes. It may have been pleasure for him, but it was torture for me. I drank water. He is all skin and bones like I was at his age. No fair!

Anyhow, after dinner we stopped by one of those big mega pet supply stores. I was in the neighborhood and I needed cat food … well, the cats needed cat food. I really don't care for the stuff except for that one brand … but that's a whole different story. So, the cats had reminded me passionately as I left the house to please return with some wet food. They still had the dry stuff, but they were not particularly satisfied by this limitation. While we were out, someone even called my cell phone from an unknown number. I didn't answer. I think it was FuzzButt calling to complain about how long it was taking.

Ok, so we stopped at the mega pet supply store and went in for cat food. Who knew this could be such an adventure? Where the heck was the Friskees and 9 Lives? There were all sorts of brands

I had never even heard about. Did you know there is certified organic cat food? One can said it was certified to be 97% tuna. It was $1.85. Now, wait a minute. I can buy a can of 100% tuna in the grocery for under a buck! I'll be damned if Fuzzbutt is eating better tuna than me! He doesn't even have a job! But what could be so special about this stuff? I also saw another can called Grammy's Homemade Stew. Why is Grammy making stew for the cats? She never made stew for me! $1.69 per can. Grammy is making a killing off of her stew! It had better be good!

After getting past the sticker shock, I decided that the cats deserved a special treat every once in a while. Will had just been treated to a shake. The cats needed to be treated to a can of "Ocean's Breeze" $1.85 cat food! They were just gonna be so happy with me for going out hunting and bringing home such a trophy dinner. Upon arriving home I marched into the kitchen and tapped the top of the can as I often do and here came Smoky running in to investigate. He sauntered up to the plate, sniffed, and then turned and attempted to cover up this "Breeze" I had brought him as if it was some thing that belonged in the litter box! You would think they would have at least tested this stuff on real cats to see if they even would eat it! I left it out overnight and this morning it was still sitting there. I dumped it in the trash. I bought four cans of this stuff. Four different flavors. I am afraid to offer the cats any more. They may incite a coup if I don't start doing my job better.

But I do have a plan to recoup my losses. It's almost 5 pm. Dinner time!

"Will! Your homemade stew is ready! It's Grammy's secret recipe!"

What Matters

I spent a few hours at an NFL game tonight. I paid ten dollars to park a mile from the stadium. I then got my exercise getting the rest of the way there. I paid $26.50 to eat sub par junk food. I had nice seats about ten rows back on the end zone. Except most of the game they seemed to play at the other end of the field. Some guy proposed to one of the cheerleaders who were in front of me. She said yes. All of the guys in the stadium were jealous. The game was close. 20-16 was the final score. Then I got more exercise getting back to my car. All in all it was a good night. Going to events like this are always a traffic nightmare and the food is always expensive and disappointing, but the getting out, going there, being a part of a fun event is worth it. Home is more comfortable, but less memorable. I love to be on the go. I am very fortunate. I have experienced so many things in my first forty-nine years. No complaints. Things don't always go as planned, but the overall picture has been a good one. There are still things I wish for, of course. Some things just don't go my way, but I keep moving. I keep going forward. I keep fighting for the things I desire and believe in.

And those things typically aren't stuff. I treasure experiences and relationships. Those are the things that make a life enriching and filling. Those are the things that matter.

—

They say the rain is coming. They say it's because of that darned hurricane they had down south. They say the whole weekend will be a washout. Shoot! I was planning on doing yard work all weekend! Now I will have to take a couple naps and watch a little TV and eat stuff that's bad for me. I may even be forced to go get a massage just to pass the time. If only I could have been out there all hot and sweaty and dirty in the yard instead. Gosh darnit anyhow!

Old Man Traits

I made a trip to the Amish grocery store yesterday. It is about an hour from home. A very cool little place. They sell bulk goods and fresh local garden fruits and vegetables, cheeses, meats, and baked goods. I spent $88 on jerky and ham salad and tomatoes and oats and sweet bologna and buckwheat, among other things. It was nice to go, but it was a busy place. I was disappointed that they were out of cinnamon bread. Somebody beat me to it, I guess.

I get amused by people. They do goofy things. I was standing in the line to check out. There were three cashiers who would simply yell for the next person in line. Along the line there are various vegetables. They had green beans and tomatoes and potatoes and peaches and such along there. This one old guy came ambling up through there inspecting the tomatoes, first the yellows, then the reds, totally oblivious that he was holding up the whole checkout process. Things came to a halt for about two minutes while he carefully made his tomato selections. Nobody said anything. They just kept hoping he would "notice". He never did. Once he had meticulously made his selections, he just ambled on his way heading back toward the sticky buns as if he were the only person in the whole store.

I think I may be starting to get some old man traits. I don't know for sure. But I do know that about once a week, while driving, some car I do not recognize will race past me and honk their horn angrily as if I must have done something wrong. I will have no clue as to why they honked, so I just smile and wave and go back to my texting.

The Five Dollar Egg

Here it is, Labor Day! But what's bugging me today is Easter. Once again I find myself wondering where that $5 egg might be. Let me explain. My yard is rolling and tree filled and surrounded by woods on two sides. I played host to an Easter egg hunt this year. There were real eggs and plastic ones filled with candy. There were also some plastic ones filled with money! That's how you get teenagers to Easter egg hunt by filling some eggs with pure cash. Some just had change, but some had dollar bills and a few had $5 bills. When all was said and done, we were still missing one real egg, and one $5 egg. I can assume that a raccoon or something found the real egg. He was probably quite surprised to find it fully cooked laying in the bushes. But where is that $5? I thought for certain at some point during the summer when mowing or trimming I would stumble across it, but no such luck. Now here it is Labor Day, the summer is coming to a close, and my five bucks is still out there. The kids gave up the hunt long ago, but I am determined! I want my money!

This reminds me of the time when I first got hearing aids. I was not used to wearing them and while outside working, I lost one! Those suckers were expensive too! We looked and looked and looked, no luck. We even bought a big magnet on wheels used on construction sites to pick up loose nails and such and Shelly spent hours out in the yard rolling that thing around hoping to find it. Still, no luck. I broke down and ordered a new one. About a month later I was walking along when I looked down and saw my hearing aid hanging in a bush. Now I have three.

Back to my Easter egg problem. I know what you are thinking. How hard can it be to find a brightly colored plastic egg, right? Uh huh ... you see, this year at the store I found the coolest things. I thought it would be such a good challenge for the kids, so I bought a dozen of them ... camouflage colored plastic eggs. That damned thing is hiding out there in plain sight. It probably snickers every time I nearly step on it! But I am telling you, if it takes me twenty years, the last laugh will be mine!

On the Tour

I am going to the PGA playoffs this weekend. I will be hanging out with Tiger and friends. I think this will be a fun outing. I think they should let me play! I will take my clubs along just in case! I hear that last place this week makes $110,000. I can live with that. I won't even complain when Tiger's ball travels twice as far as mine. Can I still have two mulligans per nine holes? Of course there is a small problem. My balls usually land right where everybody is standing. Do we need to have the stands evacuated before I tee off on each hole?

I have a vicious drive. I once hit one sideways off of the post that holds the roof on the riding cart while another golfer was sitting in the same cart. I rattled one drive under a moving car in a parking lot near the first tee of a classy course. My favorite though, is a shot I hit from 225 yards to within two feet of the hole, the wrong hole, a hole on another green, while other people were putting on that green. Would Tiger be upset if that happens this weekend? Be watching for me on TV! I will be the guy whooping and hollering as I am handed my last place check!

Hold the Broccoli

I am making turkey for dinner. No, it's not Thanksgiving. No, I don't have company coming. It's even a weeknight. I just like turkey, okay? I did not go all out with the homemade noodles and stuffing and such. But, I do have taters and corn to go with it. And before all of you women complain, nope there is nothing green to eat tonight! I will add color by breaking out a can of cranberry sauce. Don't you just hate that? You make a great tasting meal and then some health conscious female relative will come along and say, "Where's the vegetables?"

"Well, I have taters and corn … and cranberry stuff!"

"Those aren't REAL vegetables! You need something green!"

"Oh, Okay! I will put out some celery."

"Celery!!! That's no kind of vegetable!"

"Well then what is it? It sure as hell isn't a meat! Or a fruit!"

Then here it comes! They always have to break out the "B" word at about this time.

"I am talking something like Broccoli!"

See, I told you! But I DO NOT like broccoli! I don't care how much you cover it up in cheese sauce. It still tastes like broccoli!

They never say kale or spinach or guacamole, it's always broccoli! It's as if that's the only green thing out there to eat! I like avocados and peppers and lime Jell-O, but I guess they don't count even though they are just as green. So, tonight I am serving up a beautiful early September turkey dinner complete with everything needed to make it taste good! And no broccoli will be anywhere in sight!

Too Short

Days are too short anymore. I never seem to get everything done before bedtime. Here I sit. It's 10:30pm and I need another four or five hours to get caught up. The trouble is that I am already tired and getting sleepy. I cannot just force myself to stay up and get caught up because I need to be up at 7:00am to get started on tomorrow. And Lord knows I need my beauty sleep. I just cannot seem to ever get caught up. My life is always running behind. I do not know how I would react if I got caught up and looked around me and there was nothing left that needed to be done. I could then just goof off! I don't have enough goof off time now. We all need goof off time. Sometimes I take a little goof-off time, but there is always something I know that needs done, therefore cutting my goof-off time short. No fair! FuzzButt is laying over on the sofa. He does nothing but goof off most of the time. Why does he have the easy life?

OCD

I really have a difficult time understanding people sometimes. What makes them do the things they do? For example, I had lunch with a woman the other day. I have had lunch with this same woman maybe five times this year. Every time when they bring her the plate, she takes a few minutes to dissect and inspect each one of the individual ingredients within the meal. The recent meal was Mexican. She tore her burrito apart identifying lettuce and onions and chicken and peppers. There was this one little speck of green herb she did not recognize so she stopped a passing server to ask her what this was. I wanted to just reach over with my fork and stir it all together and say "Now EAT IT!"

Mrs. Clean

I was in a fast food joint for a quick breakfast the other day. While sitting and consuming my food, this woman in her sixties came along and claimed a table across the way. She took napkins and meticulously cleaned the entire table. She then placed one napkin at each of the four places. Next, she wiped down all four chairs. Finally she placed a small stack of napkins in the center of the table. All of the napkins were placed with precision to make sure they all faced the same direction. The last thing she did before taking a seat was remove her sweater and neatly fold it before placing it over the back of her chair. Shortly after she became seated with perfect posture, her husband arrived with two cups of coffee. They sat there quietly, obviously waiting for another couple to arrive. I unfortunately had to leave this fascinating scene to go to an appointment, but I left with one lasting impression. I would HATE to have to live with this woman!

Keep Moving

Someday never comes for most of us. We have all of these things that we plan to accomplish "someday". Take a trip, get a new job, move to a more exotic locale. Why are we always putting these things off? We don't put off the boring stuff so much. I have never heard someone say, "Someday I am gonna earn enough money to pay the electric bill!" No matter how outrageous the bill, we figure out a way to get it done. Why don't we have that same determination concerning the fun stuff?

It is sad to me that many dreams for many people go unrealized. Don't do that to yourself! Get out there and just do it! I am luckier than most. I have gotten to experience many remarkable things so far in my life. I have taken chances. Many times I have failed, but the triumphs make it all worth while. Fear of failure is a big reason for not chasing dreams. Failure hurts!

I am frustrated at times, let down by people at times, but I gotta keep moving. I gotta keep taking the chances and finding the treasures.

P. T. Drug Dealer

A friend of mine was out on his job delivering documents to a residence in a "not so desirable" neighborhood. His GPS was not 100% accurate and he needed to circle the block a couple of times to locate the correct address. His driving caught the attention of a police officer who came up behind him and turned on his flashing lights. My friend pulled over and awaited the officer. When the officer arrived, my friend asked what it was he had done wrong? He was informed that he was being stopped for suspicion of being in the neighborhood for the purpose of buying drugs. He was told that the house with young men standing out front was a crack cocaine house. Upon proper explanation, my friend was sent on his way with a cautionary warning to be careful.

This true story left me with a question. If the officer knew where the drug dealers were, then why were they not arresting the dealers and closing down the operation? I am baffled by his logic of chasing some guy driving in the neighborhood while letting a known crack house continue to exist. Is that just me or is that plain weird?

Elvis Moment

I look like Elvis tonight. I played racquetball with my friend earlier and he hit me in the upper lip with the ball. It left me with an Elvis sneer. I really think my friend is out to get me. In recent weeks, he has hit me in the lip, the back of the head, the boob, and he even caused me to hit myself in the forehead with my own racquet causing a bloody mess. He seems like a nice guy, but I am beginning to have my doubts. I think he may be jealous of my boyish good looks! I guess he doesn't realize that everybody cannot be as handsome as me, knocking on the doorstep of fifty. I can't help it if I still look eighteen … well, I do have some gray hairs … only a few thousand, a few extra pounds … only forty, and maybe an extra ache and pain … or thirty. I don't think anybody would notice those minor changes in me, do you?

Casket Games

Am I the only one who finds this world so amusing? Just the other day I was driving down a street on the other side of town, a street I rarely travel. I found myself highly entertained by three things. The first was a man on a bicycle. His blue jeans were too low and his shirt was too high and he was just merrily riding along totally unaware that he was mooning the world as he went. Not a plumbers moon, but a bona fide full moon. Next I saw a van parked in a vacant lot. On the side was a banner. FREE CELL PHONE! FREE MINUTES! People were lined up twenty deep to get a phone out of the back of this van. Of course I am sure there were no strings attached to this offer and the guy in the van would be right there if there is a problem. People love offers that are too good to be true. Another mile down the street sat a store. An old fashioned storefront with their wares displayed in the windows. The sign on the building said DISCOUNT CASKET STORE. Now wait a minute! Do you mean to tell me that I can get a deal on my casket? I wonder if they run Columbus Day sales! I could go ahead and pick one up and just keep it in the spare bedroom. I bet they are comfortable too. Do you think Aunt Martha would mind when she comes for a visit? And until I need it, I can roll it out into the front yard every October and scare the crap out of some neighborhood kids! Now I am getting lots of good ideas. Leave it by the side of the road and hide in the bushes to see if anybody stops and peeks inside. Or just haul it around in the back of a pickup truck to see if anybody notices. This thing could definitely be worth the price! Sneak up to the funeral home and slide it into the back of the hearse when nobody is looking. Place it in the cemetery beside a donation bucket with a sign saying, PLEASE HELP! CAN'T AFFORD A BURIAL. The possibilities are just endless!

Whined Up

I am in need of a good vacation. It's only Wednesday and the week has been about a month long already. Nothing goes as planned. Everything is an added struggle, and nobody wants to sit and listen to me whine about it! I think I will just stomp my feet and hold my breath and refuse to eat broccoli until somebody listens to me! I want my way and I want it now!

It all started innocently enough. I won my fantasy football league game to remain undefeated. Life was good! But then on Monday and Tuesday I encountered some oddballs. The kind of oddballs who hear voices telling them to do bad things and who actually listen to those voices and do them. I mean everybody has a little voice inside their head and it sometimes tells them to do bad things, like in seventh grade when it told me to pinch the butt of that girl standing in front of me in the lunch line. But, these people had voices telling them to do much bigger things, like where to go to find secret alien landing strips and such. Then I had three important business meetings in a row cancel. Then yesterday I went to the doctor for a routine check. I get to do those often since my stroke a couple years ago. Today they called and said the doc wants me to come back Friday to discuss a few things. Obviously he is needing fashion tips from me or wants to know my secret for staying so young. He probably realized that Christmas is around the corner and decided I needed a few tests run to make sure he is financially set for the holidays. So I am now in full whining mode! Deal with it!

Tell Them Often

What really matters in life? It's the relationships and time. Why is this on my mind? My oldest daughter, Shelly, has chosen not to speak to me in over a year. What started as a disagreement, got way out of hand. I miss her every day. I never would have dreamed she would be so far from me. We were always very close. I never saw this coming. I am at a point in my life where I realize that time and relationships are what matter most. Time matters because we are each given only a little of it. Time flies by like a leaf in the breeze on a Fall day. Relationships matter because they are the blending of our being; the way to reach out looking for ways to share this experience of living. My fear as I get older is that time is wasting with regard to my desire to mend the relationship with my daughter. At her age, she may not fully grasp the fact that time will soon be gone for us. I have no desire to waste even one more minute than necessary without her in my life. If she only knew how deeply I love her and how I would do just about anything for her. And all I really want in return is a little time. Never assume things are ok when it comes to those you love the most. Let them know often that they matter to you. Tell them you care. Tell them often.

Feeling Tested

I went back to see the doctor today. If you have been keeping up with me, you will know that he had requested a return visit from earlier in the week. I don't know what I did to make him want to hurt me! He started off by giving me four injections in my wrists. That was 9:30am. It is now 6:00pm and my finger-tips are still numb. He SAID this was to settle down the nerves in my hands. I think he just wanted to see a grown man cry for his mommy. On top of this, next week he wants me to have the electrocution test where they stick a needle in you in different places and then send a jolt of electricity running through it. Oh what fun! I also get to have an ultrasound and a head MRI and a 4 hour EEG brainwave study. He says these tests will check how well my brain is functioning. Heck, if he would have just asked me, I could have told him the answer to that! My brain is FULL! There is no more memory space left on my hard drive. When I learn something new, I have to forget something old, otherwise I very well may crash for the weekend. I don't always click on the correct file when retrieving information either. Sometimes I have a heck of a time finding what I am looking for in there. Do

I need to be defragmented? I certainly hope it isn't painful. But most importantly, just fix whatever is wrong in there that makes me forget where I left things. Maybe I can get him to implant a GPS chip for my car keys and TV remote. Now that would be a time saver.

Pumpkin Season

It's almost here! Just two more days! I can't wait! I am so excited! What am I so worked up about? Well, pumpkin pie season of course! Whatever the reason, you can never find a good slice of pumpkin pie other than in the months of October, November, and December. Why is that anyhow?

I have never really understood the problem. I do know that my solution is to eat a year's worth of pumpkin pie in three months to make up for the lost time. There seem to be several foods with this issue. I wonder what makes them special. Deviled eggs. I love them. I only get them at Easter dinner. Green bean casserole with those onion things. Thanksgiving. Cranberry sauce shaped like the can. Ditto.

And while we are on the subject, go ahead and tell Aunt Martha to stop trying to make some fancy dessert thing with whole cranberries every year. Just buy the can! It's what everybody wants anyhow. Sauerkraut. New Year's Day That's for me. For others, New Year's is a different food. Down south, for instance, they go for black-eyed peas and turnip greens. Another southern holiday favorite is chitlins. There are lots of others for me. I understand that your personal list may be different. For me it's homemade noodles, fresh pork side with mustard, funnel cake, and homemade pizza. Why are these foods so rare in our diet?

The Card

I am quite distraught this morning. I couldn't sleep all night. I have been upset ever since I got home yesterday and got the mail out of the mailbox. I opened the very plain looking envelope and was devastated to see the news that I have been targeted by the same cruelty that spelled the end for millions of young people who came before me. That's correct. My AARP card has arrived.

I don't know who those people are who are behind this prank! There has obviously been some mistake! I am only 18 ... again! You have to be like 50 or something to get the card! And I am NOT 50! I am nowhere near it! I still have like almost a whole month until my next birthday! Who are they to presume that I will even make it that far? Maybe I will go ahead and die young just to spite them! I am nothing like those people! People on AARP have gray hair and they take pills and vitamins and enjoy a good afternoon nap ... and grunt when they get up out of a chair and ... can't eat spaghetti for dinner ... and ... are ready for bed by 10:00 ... and ... um ... ah ... er ... sometimes forget what they were about to say ... and ... sometimes forget what they were about to say ... and ... oh ... and they repeat themselves! And I am NONE of those things! So I am gonna take that stupid card and throw it in the trash! There was obviously some mistake! Must have been a typo on my record … my what? Discounts? Senior discounts? Really? Well, ok I will put the stupid thing in my wallet so I can get cheap coffee. I don't even like coffee, but I may have to start drinking it since it is discounted. But I am NOT using that damned card for ANYTHING else! Well, maybe to save money on hotels, but that's where I draw the line!

Simplicity

I am listening to the rain tonight. It is a chilly rain. It is coming down hard enough to hear it on the roof. It is very soothing. I don't take the time often enough to pay attention to such things. It's a basic pleasure. A book and a rainstorm make good company. Like opening the windows on a cool, windy day outside and then laying down for an afternoon nap under a blanket. On a nice day, it is fun to pick out shapes in the clouds. We don't do that enough anymore. We should. It should be a priority. "Sorry Mr. Johnson, I will need to call you back. I am busy watching clouds right now."

I can make a case for simplicity in life. One night recently, we built a fire out in the side yard and cooked marshmallows half the night. Does it get any better? I am as guilty as the next guy of complicating my life too much. For example, I have a perfectly good hammock and have not used it all summer. Now that's a crime! I should use it much more than the weedeater! I am making plans for a simpler Winter. I have started chopping up firewood from an old tree I chopped down in the backyard this spring. I have a big fireplace in the basement and the animals and I are making plans to hang out down there a lot this Winter. I can sit down there all cozy and write my stories. I can have my marshmallows delivered. I won't have a need to leave the house for three months! Doesn't that sound exciting? I guess I may want to go out and play racquetball sometimes and I do still need to go to my meetings and the grocery store … and the doctor and …

Mystery to Solve

There is something funny going on here. Every night, in the middle of the night, the thermostat changes mysteriously down to sixty degrees. I have not programmed it to do so and nobody is awake to change it … except Fuzzbutt. He claims he has nothing to do with it, but he is quite the prankster and he has been kinda upset about that cat food that I bought him that is supposed to be healthy. He doesn't seem to understand that I am just trying to help him watch his figure. He seems to be of the opinion that I am just torturing him. I tried explaining that the healthy stuff is more expensive but that I bought it anyhow because I care. He said that he is not buying that line of crap and then he punctuated that statement by leaving me a hairball on my dress shoe. He said it was just an unfortunate accident, but I am not so sure I believe him. There's just a lot of tension around here these days. I am keeping the milk locked up and I don't turn my back when he is over near the knife drawer. I also noticed that he is hiding his toys where I can't find them. I really think this is unfair. I mean, I like to play too.

Duke

Will has been wanting a dog. Our old dog passed away over a year ago. He has told me how we need a new one to have around the house. I came across a dog on Friday who was in need of a home. I brought him home as a surprise. Will was very pleased. FuzzButt was NOT! He has filed a formal protest. He sees no reason to bring in such a smelly, ugly creature who eats cat food when nobody is looking and steals his spot on the sofa or my lap. And why does this mutt get to share in table scraps from dinner? FuzzButt did sneak up behind him and smell him. As soon as the dog turned around, FuzzButt hissed and spit and ran away. Our cats are not afraid of dogs. They do work to show them who is boss though. The old yellow cat came right over and laid down and went to sleep two feet from the new arrival and simply ignored him.

The dog? Oh he is a bit perplexed by these cats who don't back away when he comes ambling by. He is just a mutt. A beagle and a terrier mix. He is not a big dog. He is about 18 months old. The old yellow cat may outweigh him. I am sure they will figure out a pecking order soon enough.

Birthday Wishes

Well, it's about two weeks until my big birthday. I will turn fifty on Halloween. I knew you were probably struggling with what to buy me, so I thought I had better give you a list of ideas.

Let's start with headphones. I broke the ones I use with my Nook. I slept on them and they got rolled up under me and the wire broke right up at the earpiece. Those were good ones and I had won them for free. I also want that cookies n cream fried ice cream from the place up by the mall. Somebody mentioned to me about Dessert Day and I have been craving that ever since. Speaking of which, I would like my very own pumpkin pie … and a fork. A new cable remote would be nice. Only half the buttons currently work on mine. They are free up at the cable company, but I never think of it when I am not watching TV. A new spindle for the riding mower. It's only like $18 and if you really want to see me happy you can install it too. I was mowing last week and the iron manhole cover just jumped right up out of the ground and got tangled in my blades. I have no clue how that happened. I need one black cotton sock. One of mine has a hole in it, so I don't need a pair, just a single replacement. I don't really care if it's an exact match. Nobody will notice anyway. Toenail clippers. Can't find mine anywhere. Maybe that's why my sock has a hole in it. Pillows. I like lots of pillows to sleep with. I get a bunch and they always seem to disappear. A toaster that will hold an elongated piece of bread. I hate having a toaster where you buy healthy bread and then have to toast one side and then turn it over and do the other. By then the first side is cold! That's at least my starter list. I will try to get back to you with the rest later.

Just My Opinion

How do you feel about things? Are you against immigrants? How do you feel about Gay and Lesbian couples? Mexicans? African Americans? Polish? What about Muslims? I am not talking about the extremists, just Muslims in general. Do you have a thing against Catholics? Presbyterians? Do you hate White people? Maybe you despise cat lovers. Red hair. Does it just drive you up the wall? Maybe it's women who don't shave their legs. Perhaps it's those people who come to your door handing out literature about their faith. Mormons? Seventh Day Adventists? Jehovah's Witnesses? What about Democrats? Republicans? Libertarians? How do you feel about Jews? How many of these groups of people do you wish would just disappear? Well, who gave you the right to judge anybody?

Let's knock these down one at a time. I am sure that some American Indians would prefer that nobody, including your great grandparents, had ever immigrated to America. If you are reading this book, then you are most likely the offspring of immigrants. You were just lucky enough to be born here. I don't think any of us got to choose where we were born . We were either lucky or not.

Gay and Lesbians. Do you want someone to dictate what you do in the bedroom? Well, then get your nose out of theirs. You certainly wouldn't want someone who believes differently than you telling you how to conduct your love life, so you worry about yourself and let them do the same.

Mexicans? Many of them that I have known simply come here in search of a better life. Just because you were lucky enough to be born into it, does that give you some special pass to have more?

African Americans? Hell their ancestors didn't even come here by choice! Then their descendants were treated as second class citizens for generations. No wonder they have struggled as a people. I wonder how kindness and acceptance might work.

Polish? It may sound silly today, but the older generations made many degrading remarks about this group of people who were merely seeking a better life.

Muslims? Granted, there is a radical faction, but most Muslims are peace-loving people who simply worship a different religion. Isn't that their choice? Their right? Christianity has radical factions too. Klansmen consider themselves to be Christian. Does that make all Christians Klansmen? I mentioned Mormons ... again, just a variation on religion. There is an offshoot of the Mormons that believes in polygamy, but their mainstream church does not.

Do the Seventh Day Adventists and Jehovah's Witnesses deserve your hate and scorn just because their religious beliefs differ from yours? Do you want someone telling you how you should believe? I bet not. The same is true of any religion. Shouldn't every person get to choose their own path?

Do you really deserve to hate somebody just because of political or religious beliefs or their ethnicity? I am only one man with one opinion, but why not just take care of your own backyard and let the others in this world do the same. We are all on this little speck of a planet together. Hate is ugly. Hate is never productive. Judgment is ugly. Where did I hear that?" judge not lest ye be judged?" Hmm Funny how people selectively decide what to believe and what not to believe.

That's my rant for the day. Now just go out and be nice to one another in spite of your differences. You might be amazed at what happens!

My Purpose

I am tired tonight. No good reason, just tired. No overexertion, no long hours slaving over some project, just want to go to bed early. I was up at seven thirty this morning, got dressed and went to a meeting. That lasted maybe an hour. I then made a few phone calls and ran an errand or two before lunch. I then did a little paperwork and chatted with an old friend while it rained this afternoon. My day ended with breakfast for dinner. Now, here I sit. You would think I labored intensely all day. I am just a blob. I do have a sinus headache, a slight one. But nothing serious. I even got my annual test results back from the doctor today. He ordered an MRI of my head and ultrasound of my neck. I do indeed have a brain! Regardless of what some may say. And it is healthy! Now if I only knew what to do with that healthy brain. I did have a plan for the next forty-nine years, but that fell through. Now, I am trying to find my purpose. What if I don't have one? I mean, does everyone have a purpose? What if I forgot to get in the purpose line at the factory? Are some people meant to just wander through life? I could be good at that! I am also good at starting things, I just need to find someone good at finishing all of my projects.

—

Today was one of my favorite days of the year. It was crisp this morning, sunny and warm by afternoon, a moderate breeze. The combination meant it was raining leaves. I love the thought that after spending its whole life stuck to a tree, a leaf spends its final grand moment in flight and I love when I am there to witness this event. I think we all should be able to end our lives in a free flight like that. A carefree journey to our final resting place.

Graced by My Beauty

Why am I here? What is my purpose in life? I know I keep asking those questions a lot. That's because I haven't truly figured that out yet. And what if the time for my purpose already passed, but I was at the golf course that day? What then? Then again, maybe golf is my purpose! Maybe I am here to bean someone important in the head with a golf ball at just the right moment! I could be good at that! I once hit a ball sideways and nearly took off the head of my playing partner sitting in the cart. I am not the worst though … one of my friends once hit a tee shot that landed behind him. It went straight in the air with so much spin that he got negative net yards.

Maybe my purpose has to do with music. I've played a few thousand shows over the years. Maybe one of those had important meaning in the life of someone. I bet it was my singing! Someone was probably touched the time I dressed up as Olivia Newton-John and did a lip sync performance of "Let's Get Physical". Or perhaps it was the time we accidentally set an outhouse on fire during a show. Or maybe the time we showed up at this place where the stage was enclosed in chicken wire for our safety.

I suppose it could be my writing … nah. I don't see peanut butter and pickles changing the world … well … you know … come to think of it … the first call I ever received from my publisher was from a young woman who said she wanted to learn more about peanut butter and pickles!

I know what it is! I am here to grace the world with my handsomeness! It is my job to just stand around and look pretty and I am damned good at it! I am glad I finally figured this out! I am going down to the mall right now and stand right out in the middle where everyone can behold my beauty!

Too Much Relaxing

I enjoy quiet time, but I am too anxious to enjoy it. Does that make sense? I look forward to having the time to relax in peace, but I cannot seem to just sit still and do nothing. I am just fidgety all of the time. I always need to be doing something. Usually it is two or three things at the same time. Right now, for instance, I am home alone. I should sit quietly. Not a chance! I will sit for a minute, then decide I need a drink, sit down again, then decide the dog needs to go outside, sit another minute, remember that I need to throw in a load of laundry, return to the couch, decide I now need a snack to go with my drink, back to the couch, now my drink is empty again and I now have food, couch again, oops, the damned dog is still outside, couch, do I hear the toilet still running in the bathroom, couch, where did I leave my phone in case somebody is looking for me, couch, clothes need to go in dryer, couch, start a load of dishes too, couch, have you seen the nail clippers, couch, damn this relaxing is hard work!

Visiting Memories

Here I sit. My day is winding down. I am at home. There is a cat stretched out on the sofa next to me. There is a dog on the floor at my feet chewing on one of those artificial bones you can buy at the store. It was a warm Fall day here so the house felt a bit stuffy. I didn't want to turn on the AC, so I turned on a fan instead. Aside from the animals, I am home alone. It is quiet, only the sound of the fan, which I find kind of soothing. The entryway light is the only one on and it has gotten dark outside. I feel comfortable entombed in my own little world. Outside of these walls everything imaginable is going on all at once. Somebody is being born and somebody is dying. Someone is happy and someone is sad. Someone is doing good and someone is doing bad. It's all out there. Every minute of every day. Everything all at once is happening somewhere. The world is a busy place. It is nice to unplug from it for a moment or two.

For me, I am always curious about the lives of others. We each have our own path through this world and while we share so much commonality, we also have many differences. That's what keeps it fun! It's never all as we would want it, but it's surely an adventure.

Change is both the good and the bad part of it. For me, the bad part is probably the people I have lost along the way. Some passed on, some moved on, some disowned me, and some just drifted. I miss the best of what I shared with each of them. I make new friends along the way, but I wish I could keep the old ones close as well. I can deal with the growing older and the changing times and new adventures, I just wish I didn't need to lose the past.

I would give anything to hear Pap say "Hoyt" (that means Hi) or to play Frisbee with Shelly, to pig out at Denny's with Annie, or to walk down the Ronson Hill Road with dad again. To see Will's excitement when I would bring him home a new dinosaur, or to spend a day in the woods with Curt, to make a big leaf jumping pile with the kids down the road, or to feel the pride inside when I saw Elizabeth perform her music for the first time.

Don't ever lose those things. They are all right there in your mind. Pay them a visit from time to time. Keep them alive through your memories.

—

There is a cold wind blowing outside tonight. I am lucky. I am several hundred miles from the storm causing the problem. The worst thing I had to do was retrieve a garbage can and take the dog out to pee. He got his business done quickly tonight! No goofing around smelling everything or trying to see what the neighbor's dog was up to. He was back inside and curled up on the couch in a flash. I wasn't far behind him. I even bought some cocoa at the store the other day. I am in the mood to make some of the real stuff, not that instant imitation crap. I even have some big marshmallows out there in the kitchen. What a great night! And it's Monday, so there is a football game on! Have I died and gone to heaven? I don't even have to be out of bed early tomorrow! I can barely stand all of this excitement!

Happy Fifty

Well, here it is! October 31st, 2012 is upon us! My personal half century mark! I honestly am gonna need a little more time than just one mere century to get everything done that I have already started. I don't know if you have noticed, but there's a lot to do around this world! I could probably spend the next ten years just sorting through all of the treasures out in the Mancave. Fifty years. Wow! But fifty good years. I have been so blessed and so lucky to have lived the life I have lived so far. I have gotten to experience more than I could have dreamed. It's not all fluffy and happy either, but it's all been worth the struggles along the way. Like the song says, "regrets too few to mention". The best thing is the people who have touched my life. That is what I cherish and also miss the most; the people. The relationships. From a very young age through the present, my memories of this life are filled with wonderful people who gave that life quality and character. So, here I go bounding forward into the next fifty with all of the anticipation and excitement of a little kid. Lots more mistakes to make, challenges to tackle, mountains to climb, and people to meet!

—

Now wait a minute! Will had me to spend $40 at the Halloween costume store so that he could run all over the neighborhood and collect $10 worth of candy. Then I spent another $15 on candy to give out to other kids who showed up at my house. $55. What if next year I just give Will $15 worth of candy and then I will go out and get myself some dinner with the other $40! Everybody wins!

Concession

I am conceding the 2012 election. My campaign failed to gain traction beyond my living room. My $4.95 advertising budget just failed to get the message out there. I am devastated. I am, however, available to take a cabinet position in the administration. I hear the pay and perks are pretty good. I also would consider being U.S. ambassador to Fiji or the Cayman Islands. It is the least I can do for my country. I am a good guy like that. Ambassador to Iceland? Iran? Darnn it! I have prior engagements preventing me from accepting those positions. I do know of a couple of people I might recommend for those assignments. Again, just trying to help out in a non-partisan way. I do wish to make one further announcement this evening. I am using this moment to announce my candidacy for the 2016 election. I want to get off to a strong start. You can be a part of this grass roots effort.

Felined

Me and the old yellow cat are just hanging out this afternoon. It is a beautiful, sunny day and warm for mid November. I have gotten my errands done and when I got home I opened several windows to let that sweet fall air inside. It's just about perfect out there. The yellow cat is a funny one. She must be about 14 or so, but she is in fairly good shape, other than weighing probably 12 or 13 pounds. She enjoys hanging out with me, but doesn't want to sit on me like the others. She prefers to just be near me on the arm of the chair or up above me on the back of the sofa. She is actually Shelly's cat, but somehow I still seem to be the one feeding her. Will calls her the freeloader cat because she is the only one living here without an owner. She never eats with the other cats, never has. She always prefers to wait until they are all finished, then take her turn. I don't know how she ended up being the biggest of them all. Of course Fuzzbutt is the smallest and eats like a pig. Makes no sense. The old yellow one also prefers dry food rather than canned. Her only exception is turkey. She might just eat the whole bird in one sitting if given the opportunity.

Where is everybody else? Well, I am the only human at home. The other cats are perched in windows and such around the house. The dog is outside sniffing everything to make sure he knows who has been here recently. There won't be anybody else here until 7:30pm when Will gets off work. He has followed in his sisters footsteps working at the little Italian place up the road. He, like them, enjoys making some extra spending money.

The black cat just came walking through. She looks funny these days. She and Fuzzbutt had a big argument a couple weeks ago and it seems Fuzzbutt bit off a piece of her ear. It's just a little piece, but she still looks a bit funny. I think she thinks it makes her look tough. What is funny is that Fuzzbutt is a big chicken and was just trying to get away. I bet he is telling the other cats in the neighborhood a different story.

Getting Fat

I am washing clothes, washing dishes, and cooking right now. Actually, I am sitting on the sofa while machines do the work for me. Isn't it funny how we complain about these chores? Just think what was involved a hundred years ago in accomplishing these tasks. We are so lucky! And so lazy! Soon I will be folding clothes while watching football on TV and I will be eating a meal I didn't have to grow or hunt or husk or skin or disembowel. All I had to do was haul it home from a store down the road and throw it in the oven. And don't forget, oh my God, I have to put the dishes in the cabinet from the dishwasher! Yet, at the end of the day, I will claim to be tired and ready for bed. No wonder we are all getting fat!

No Rush

I am ready for the Thanksgiving holiday. No, not Christmas. Not yet! Slow down people! Take the time to enjoy Thanksgiving first! Those poor retail workers. This year most of those stores are opening Thursday evening to start the Black Friday shopping. They obviously do not care about their employees. I am also willing to bet that the top executives will not be in the office Thursday either. I believe that whoever decided this schedule was a good idea should be working those hours too. We are in such a rush. We rarely take time to enjoy the moment. We are always rushing ahead to the next big moment. What will I do Thursday? Well, I will cook and eat, read a book etc. … Friday? I will eat leftovers and tinker at home. I love to tinker. Saturday? Maybe go to a movie. Sunday? Relax, watch football. Then, maybe, next week I can begin to plan for the month of December. No rush. I now try to enjoy the moments along the way before they are all gone. No need to rush. The next big thing will be here soon enough. Right now all I need to do is worry about turkey and pumpkin pie and cranberry sauce. That's it.

Worth the Pain

I am all achy tonight. First of all, I have been having a lot of nerve pain in my right arm for the past week. Nothing serious, just annoying. Then, last night I went and played racquetball with my friend. Now the muscles in my arm are sore too. The important thing is that after two hours of intense battle, I won four games to one. That makes the pain worth it. The place we play is a big, open exercise place. The racquetball courts run along the one side. The rear wall is some sort of clear glass so that people can see in while they walk by. They get to watch two sweaty old men in shorts chase a little ball around. I noticed several of the pretty, young women walking by appeared a bit nauseated. It was big fun for me. I moved with the grace of an elephant around the court. I displayed the speed and prowess of a koala bear. I played smart. I hit the ball where my friend wasn't and made him run his butt off. In the end I think I just wore him down.

Cherish

It's Black Friday. Shopping? No way. The best deals will be a week from Tuesday during the morning hours when the stores are empty, although I must admit that much of my shopping is being done online, so I should have it easy this year. This is a unique day for me. I have not left the house nor do I intend to. I went out in the yard and brought in some firewood from the back patio. Does that count? That doesn't mean that I have been laying on the couch all day either. I don't sit still very well. As you may know, I turned fifty recently, but I do not act or feel like it. I refuse to grow up. I know many were shocked at how good looking I still am for my advanced years. It's the Handsomers Disease. It gets worse every time I look in the mirror. Some people will themselves or resign themselves into old age. I know people my age using a cane or walker without good reason or they live to tell people about their aches and troubles and spend half their life going to the doctor. Now, I have gone to my share of doctors appointments since the stroke two years ago, but that is mostly preventative stuff. I still chase kids around the yard and play basketball and racquetball and ride my road bicycle. I still like to go fast down a big hill. I do show some signs of aging. I am never quite sure which direction my first three steps out of bed will take me, but otherwise I am lucky. I am blessed with more than I deserve. I have made many mistakes along life's path. I cannot change that which has already occurred. I will make many mistakes in the future. I am human. That is normal. For me it's all about making the most out of every day. I refuse to waste my life in bitterness or anger. If something goes wrong, the sooner you can forgive and move forward, the better. That is why I smile every day. I don't really know why I am here, but I am sure happy to be here cherishing every moment!

Old Friends

People have been after me for years to join Facebook. Over Thanksgiving weekend I finally broke down and got with the times. I have been learning how to use it ever since. I guess it's kinda cool. It's a way to stay in touch. I do have one small problem with it however. Everybody I used to know has gotten old! They are all like old men and women! Why? I mean this OBVIOUSLY has not happened to me! I am still a young, handsome devil! I went to school with a bunch of elderly people! I bet they are all on AARP! They probably all drink coffee on a senior discount at McDonalds and ask for the senior menu at Denny's. Me? I am barely out of kids meals. They go to the Y and use the Silver Sneakers program. I play racquetball and do spinning. No way I am in the same class with them! I bet they grunt when they get up from a chair … well actually I do that one. And I bet they are getting wrinkles around their … oh, I have that one too. And they probably take enough pills that it qualifies as dinner … I guess I have that one as well … But at least I still haven't found my … oh, God! No! It can't be!

—

Mom: "You're not going to the store looking like that are you?"

Me: "No mom, I am taking my good clothes with me and changing in the car. I wouldn't want to get a stain on them before I get there and become an embarrassment to you. And, yes, I put on clean underwear in case I get in an accident. Those darned doctors always seem to check that first."

Doctor: "Don't even bother prepping this one for surgery. He has pee stains on his boxers."

Problem Solved

Have you ever noticed that when a man completes a project, a woman will soon show up and find fault with the results? I once put a new laminate floor in the entryway of the house. It looked 10,000% better than the old wood tiles that I replaced. Sally comes along when I have finished and was totally obsessed with one little spot where there was some give to it! I knew the spot was there. I simply needed to ponder on the best solution for a while. Heck, it might even have come to me during the football game that was about to begin on TV! These things take time you know. I knew that at some point in the next year or two I would get back around to fixing that spot with a good plan. Yet every time Sally walked across that spot she would pause and press it with her foot. A couple of football games later I came up with a good idea and took care of the problem. I took one of Sally's socks and stuffed it up under there. See, problem solved! I was also highly entertained watching her search for a missing sock for the next few days.

Smart Cookie

I am one smart cookie. I stopped in a mall to pick up a couple of Christmas items today. It is December 18th, it is a Tuesday. I went at 10:00am. The mall was empty. See, I could stop the story right there and you would be singing the praises of my wisdom.

Let us go back three days. Three kids asked me to go to the mall. It was Saturday afternoon, December 15th. I was NOT so smart. I said ok, let's go. I had a craving for a big pretzel. I was fortunate. I found parking only one county over. That old lady with the handicap sticker had no skills. I ducked in that spot before she even knew what hit her. The mall was filled with a flowing sea of people. The kids were there to shop ... poor kids. I was just there for my pretzel and then I could just hang out while I waited on them. I made my way through the crowd down the long hallway. I had arrived at the pretzel store. As the sea of people parted, I was confronted by a line! There was a line for a pretzel! It resembled the line at Disney world for Space Mountain in mid July. It started somewhere past where I had parked my car! I tried to cut in about halfway back but there was that old handicapped woman I had seen earlier in the parking lot! I got scared. I decided I wasn't so much in a mood for a pretzel after all.

But today that old woman was nowhere in sight and there were no people in line. My pretzel tasted wonderful.

My Magical Universe

I was driving down the road today enjoying the rare warm sunshine coming through the window. Mid-January doesn't produce many days like this around here. I got to thinking about how amazing it is that any of this even exists. I looked around me and felt very small. Everything from the warm sunshine to the planet just filled with all sorts of plant and animal life and then all of the resources that we humans have molded and manipulated into this world in which we live. It is nothing short of amazing. We have much to be proud of. Just as an ant might take pride in his anthill or a spider in its web, we are merely a speck in the universe, but a complex, intricate speck. I am reminded of how ignorant I am. Because either all of this just magically appeared or has always been here or else all of this was created by a supreme being who either magically appeared or has always been here. Either way, I do not have the ability to wrap my head around the whole thing. However, I do consider myself lucky, very lucky to have the chance to experience this magnificent universe.

Not Funny

I haven't felt funny recently … let me rephrase that. I haven't felt that I have been inspired to write my usual funny stories recently. There, that's better! I feel that my stories have been less entertaining and more philosophical or informational. I want to be funny again! I know lots of true, funny stories. Why am I not writing them? I need to get back to the basics of what started me writing in the first place. All I need to do is pay attention out in the world. Take today for instance, in the grocery store parking lot I saw a man lugging his 1 year old in one arm and grocery bag in the other. The baby had its coat unzipped and hood down. It was about twenty degrees. All I could think was that I hoped for that poor man's sake that his wife didn't find out! Women bundle that baby up! Men think, "Hey it's only thirty seconds to the car and besides what kind of germ lives in twenty degree weather?" Then there was this Mexican joint where I ate my lunch. Two servers, white teenaged girls, out of four had what could best be described as metallic light blue hair. What made them think that this would be a good look? Was it on clearance at the hair color store so they said what the hell let's go for it? To follow this up, I stopped at a store to buy some new brown dress socks to replace the ones that have disappeared. Let me clarify, I still have three brown socks. None of them have a twin. I have no clue. Kids are wearing mismatched socks to school these days. As soon as adults pick up on this fad I will be soooo ready! Now, where was I? Oh! Back to the sock store. There was a woman there sporting black hair with rainbow bangs. Red, blue, green, and yellow stripes. She was about 40 in ratty mismatched clothes, out of shape, but strutting those bangs baby!

The Bare Facts

One thing about my writing is that I try to tell only positive, uplifting, or funny stories. Sometimes that creates a unique challenge since all of my stories are also true. Also, I try not to tell stories that could be harmful or hurtful to others. Again, this can be limiting. There are some great stories and funny stories that will need to be published after I am long gone from this world or else once I am old enough that I no longer care who reads them. For instance, I cannot in good conscience at this time write about the naked guy who lost his pillow somewhere in the kitchen. I also cannot discuss what really happened to that pretzel nugget at the mall. Nor can we have a conversation about … well heck, I can't even think of a way to give you a hint about that one! Actually, I think I will go ahead and tell you about the lost pillow …

I was training a new girl how to do what I do for a living besides writing. We were visiting a 70-year-old woman at her home and this was to be the first time that my trainee did most of the talking. As we approached the house I told Marie to go ahead and lead the way and I would just be a mouse in the corner so to speak.

Marie knocked and the sweet old lady, who was expecting us, opened the door and said come on in and have a seat! We walked into a living room that was part of an open floor plan with an adjacent dining room. All was nicely decorated if a bit dated as you would expect in the home of an older person. The one unexpected piece of décor was the forty something year old totally naked man standing about where the living and dining rooms met. As we entered the room, he calmly reached for a pillow from the back of the sofa and stood there silently holding it, well, strategically. My poor trainee was stopped dead in her tracks.

"Go ahead and have a seat!", the old woman said joyfully, apparently unaware of the scene behind her.

My trainee and I were seated facing the old woman on her L-shaped sofa. It was quite a sight with the spectacle behind her. I took over exchanging pleasantries as I could see my trainee was just a bit flustered.

"What a lovely home. I love what you have done with the place!"

"How is the family?"

"This looks like a great place to hang out!"

Along about this time, the pillow wielding stranger turned and walked across the dining room and disappeared into the kitchen in all of his glory.

My trainee, seeing that the crisis had passed, was able to regain her composure and began to discuss the intended purpose of our visit. That was good for about three minutes.

At that point the stranger reemerged from the kitchen walked across the dining room and returned to stand in the exact same spot as before. But, there was one difference. He had lost his pillow! And my trainee had now lost the ability to speak in comprehendible sentences.

"um er ah when um whoo oh my ..."

I knew this time she was through! I had to jump in and take over and save the day!

I proceeded to talk about the important matters at hand while avoiding any thoughts of this silent figure scratching himself in the distance. It was not an easy task. Especially with my trainee hyperventilating on the sofa beside me. After what seemed like an eternity, Mister Scratchy disappeared down the hallway toward the bedrooms.

Things from there got a bit calmer. We had a nice visit. At the end the lady said that what we were proposing sounded wonderful. She just wanted to discuss it with her children before making a final decision. I agreed and asked if they lived locally. She stated that they all lived out of town with the exception of Tommy, who lived with her.

She then said, " I am surprised that he is not out here. He usually comes out when we have company!"

My trainee quickly spoke up fearing she might yell down the hall for him to make another "appearance", "Oh it's ok, he is probably busy and we wouldn't want to disturb him. You discuss this with your kids and get back to us." As she was saying this she was hurriedly making her way to the door.

Needless to say, my trainee did not last very much longer in the business.

Solved

Amazing! Truly amazing! I have PROVEN the mystery of a lifetime! The other night I needed to wash a particular pair of pants and a shirt for an event. Into the washer I placed one pair of pants, one shirt and two socks. When I moved them to the dryer, I had one pair of pants, one shirt, and one sock! That damned washer DOES eat socks! I always suspected, but could never prove it! A great mystery of life solved by little ol' me! I am now feeling spunky! I am ready to take on more new, exciting challenges. I am making a list of those other things which have bugged me for years. Here are a few of the things I intend to find out in the coming years. Where does the cat hide all of those little plastic things off the milk jug? Who is the person that decided a mechanically separated chicken was a good source of food? What's the secret Victoria is keeping? Can I really make $1000/week doing any job advertised on a handwritten sign along the side of the road? I will keep you posted!

Lazy FuzzButt

I am cleaning house. My house is never clean, but I am cleaning house again. I am just taking a break at the moment. I scrubbed the kitchen counters and threw away a big stack of accumulated junk mail. I loaded the dishwasher and swept the floor. I then vacuumed the upstairs living room and hallway and swept the entryway. Next come the bathrooms and my bedroom. I don't know who makes all of these messes! It must be Fuzzbutt. He has a guilty look on his face. My bedroom has my clothes thrown everywhere and a water bottle collection and drink glasses on the headboard. I am a busy guy. I just come in and go to bed.

Is there a big party here during the day or something? There appear to be fingerprints on the television screen. I never touch that TV. I use the remote. Wait, maybe those are paw prints! I don't think FuzzButt is very good with the remote. Maybe he is the culprit. I also found a hairball on one of my pillows. I know it's not mine. Wrong color! I bet that lazy bum is laying in my bed all day with a big glass of milk watching Animal Planet!

Douglas

Elizabeth's boyfriend, Douglas, is a nice guy. I would have never dreamed of being able to say that about someone dating one of my kids. I always thought it would be hard for me to see anyone as "good enough". I expected to find fault in some way. But, in this case, from the very beginning, Douglas and I have gotten along just fine. I have no idea how long she and he will be together. No idea if this is long term or not. All I know is that she has chosen well. She chose someone with character and personality who is real. He pitches in and helps out. They also hang out with Will frequently. He just "fits" in our family. Significant others can sometimes create distance or a wedge in a family. I am very happy that in this case that is certainly not the case. I am not one who frequently expresses my internal feelings on such matters, but Douglas, I for one am glad to have you around.

Humbled

In Indiana and several other states there is a discount grocery store that does things on the cheap. A friend of mine, who was new to the area, went to check out this place. She became quite upset when she went to get a shopping cart and found that they were all locked up together! She went inside to get the manager. She complained to him that they needed to unlock some more carts for the customers and that this was ridiculous! He then took her over and showed her how to unlock a cart. He showed her how you deposit a quarter which is returned to you when you return the cart, therefore eliminating the cost of hiring cart boys. She humbly ate her crow and went on about her shopping.

Glen

I never use a person's real name in my stories, but in this one case I am going to make an exception. I am certain that Glen would not mind and probably even be honored. I met Glen in probably early 2007. He was one of those uniquely unforgettable characters that come along in life who are simply cast from their own mold. Glen was probably 41 years old at the time and was a cart guy and loader for a large home improvement store. At that point, he had probably already been pushing those carts for a solid eight years. He was a bit rough around the edges. A scruffy beard and curly hair stuffed up under a baseball cap, thick wire framed glasses, saggy jeans and a big belly. Take away that belly and he was actually fairly skinny. Glen was a self described slow learner. He had certain limits. He was often misunderstood for this reason. People would sometimes be mean to him or mistreat him unfairly. He really just wanted to fit in and be a part of everything in life.

Glen and I became friends. I saw in him a good guy who didn't mean harm to anybody. I admired that. He and I would meet for lunches, he even came to the house a few times for events and he even stayed at my house and took care of the animals when I was gone on a trip to New York City. He was always texting me and asking how the kids or the animals were doing. He cared plus he just wanted conversation. One of my favorite things was the question he always asked me.

"Are you my best buddy?" he would say. I was always amused at how he asked this backward from how most people would have phrased the question. I would always assure him that, yes, I was his best buddy and he was always content in knowing that fact.

Glen lived with his parents. He said it was mainly because he was not so good at managing his money. He would often go places with them and then text me and tell me about the food. He also was quite independent and would go out and meet friends on a regular basis. He was not a drinker, but he was always at Hooter's one night a week. He also went to karaoke bars and would get up and sing. He didn't have a great voice but he loved to be a part of the action. I actually had a mobile studio here at the house for awhile. One day he came by and I recorded him doing a music video and put it onto a DVD for him. I believe he was very proud of it.

It was all about the food for Glen. He absolutely loved to eat. He would often go with his parents to the casino, not because of the gambling, but for the all you can eat buffet. The boy could put away some grub I tell ya. Frequently I would meet him somewhere for lunch and an hour after I had left, he would still be there polishing off his meal. It was a good thing he pushed those carts or more than his belly would have been big!

The one thing with which Glen didn't have but probably wanted more than anything else in the world, was a girlfriend. His unkempt manner and social skills surely played a role, but also the fact that he was in his forties and only saw twenty year olds as desirable. He just didn't think women his age were that pretty!

This was part of his childlike charm. He simply spoke the truth as he knew it. He wanted a woman half his age and she had to be a knockout! Of course those girls rarely even gave him the time of day. It was a troubled part of his life which he talked with me about often but for which I had no answers to give him.

Glen remained my friend through marriage and divorce and kids growing up and moving away. He was always a part of my life. He would enjoy getting together for dinner and a movie or lunch and conversation or breakfast and a recording session. The key was that meetings with Glen always had to involve food. Like I said, this boy could eat! I sometimes would try to encourage him to make better food choices. I would tell him he wasn't getting any younger. He would always just brush it off and tell me about someone who ate bad things and lived to be ninety.

The following is a text conversation I had with Glen on December 30, 2013 …

Glen: Lynn when u feel dizzeds and fell down and on the forehead is sweeting is that bad buddy because it just happen to me

Me: Yes you should be checked out by a doctor to see if it's serious or not

Glen: Want kind of septions could that be lynn

Me: Could be something simple like ear infection or something major like heart trouble or blood pressure trouble

Glen: My ears are kind of ring and have lot of muse that ive been spiting out alot in the last week buddy

Me: Sounds like a sinus infection. Go see doctor

Glen: Ok how can u tell buddy

Me: Just my guess based on what you tell me. I am not a doctor

Glen: Do u think its because i work outside all the time and no help with the carts buddy

Me: No. You probably got it in the break room from somebody that was sick

Glen: And im getting kind cold chills now budy and my ears feel funny now some drinage now

Me: The doctor can help

Glen: Well a lot of peple on the front line and there kids to buddy and a head cashiers

Me: Yep. This time of year. Let me know what doctor says. Good night

Glen: Goodnight buddy

Those were the last words I ever heard from Glen. The next day while traveling in the car with his parents on their way to dinner, Glen suffered a massive heart attack. Despite all of the medical efforts, Glen passed away January 2, 2014 at the age of forty-eight.

I miss my best buddy.

Lesson Learned

And now as Paul Harvey would say, the rest of the story …

Losing my good friend has had an impact on me. I have sometimes wondered what if I had been more assertive and made him go to the doctor? Would he still be alive today? I will never know. I can tell you however, that I will never make that mistake again!

I have a close friend with whom I talk and text. I knew her as a kid but thanks to the internet we can now keep in contact. She told me in a text yesterday morning that she didn't feel great. She had been up and down in the night, couldn't get a full breath and her chest was tight. She also felt nauseous and had not eaten breakfast because of it. I could sense that she had every intention of playing wait and see with this. I was having no part of it! I bugged and bugged and bugged the crap out of her until she called her doctor's office. I don't think she gave them the details of her issue because they told her they could see her sometime next week. Nope, sorry, not good enough! I annoyed the hell out of her until yesterday around noon she went to an urgent care center. She explained her symptoms and they immediately referred her to the emergency room at the hospital. Was I being a pain in the ass? Yes! Do I regret it? No! The hospital, upon running some tests, decided there was enough reason to admit her to spend the night. This morning she is undergoing testing. I am hoping and assuming she will be fine. I know I was a pain in her butt. But at least I know that she will be alive for me to be a pain in her butt again tomorrow!

In Glen's passing, he taught me a valuable lesson that I will never forget.

Hairy Mess

I had a woman complaining to me about hair today. She said that men are blessed with such naturally beautiful hair and do nothing for it, while women have to pay big bucks for the same results. She then showed me a couple of photos. I think it was Kenny G and Michael Bolton. I don't know who ever said that those two were real men, but those are the two she chose. I feel reasonably certain that they have their hair (and nails and makeup) done just like women. They are more girly than most of us.

Now I will admit that some men (like me) are just naturally beautiful. No makeup, no manicures, no pedicures, no special hair products. I just roll out of bed looking good baby! It's just a God given gift!

My hair is naturally curly if I let it grow long enough and it has just a pinch of gray … well, okay, it used to be just a pinch … now it's more like, well, yes my daughter did say to me jus1 this evening that there are no brown hairs left up there! She even suggested using L'Oreal on me and she was serious! She wants to color my hair and Will wants to help! They were discussing options as if I was some hopelessly difficult science project.

I am game. I told them to bring it on! Nothing that they can do will detract from my natural handsomeness! I just think that my own children are jealous of my fantastic looks and the fact that I don't even have to work at it! I think they are just trying to ugly me up! Ain't happening! Some people are just beautiful no matter what you do to them!

Now, where was I ? Oh yes, women's hair. Women think that men have better hair, but really it's just that women need something to complain about. They always are saying how easy us guys have it. Okay girls, I am a single man right now. I know it's hard to believe! I am just exploring my options from the countless vixens knocking at my door. Anyhow, do you realize how difficult it is as a single man to keep yourself looking this good? We men do have to do a few little things. I will admit to that. I want you girls to try or at least pretend to try ... well, actually, some of you could do this for real ... but try to shave your own back hair and neck hair and ear hair and nose hair. It ain't easy! I might entertain keeping a woman who was good with a razor around just for that purpose. Well, she might need to cook and clean too ... and do the laundry ... and maybe mow the grass ... and clean out the gutters sometimes. But hey, she gets to hang around with a natural beauty like me!

Operation FuzzButt

Greetings humans! This is FuzzButt filing my latest update on life in this looney place I reside. I really have never quite figured out how this happened. You see, I have papers! I am what you call a pedigree. I am royalty in the feline world. All I remember is one day when I was young, they kidnapped me from my siblings and drugged me. Next, they put me in the cargo hold of a plane! Can you believe that? This is why I believe that I am a victim of kidnapping. What other reason would there be to put someone of my societal stature in cargo? I deserve first class!. When I woke up I was in Kentucky! Can it get any worse? This nice blonde haired lady took me in my portable jail cell on a long car ride back to her place. When we got to her house, she locked me in a bathroom and waited on the crazies to arrive. There were three little ones and a big ugly one. He is the one they call my owner. Are you kidding me? Do they not realize who I am? I heard them saying I was a birthday gift and that my name was FuzzButt. I am severely traumatized by this name. If my siblings ever heard about it, I would surely be the laughingstock of my kingdom!

From Kentucky I was then moved to a place called Tennessee to live with the crazies. Oh My God! They had mere commoner cats with whom I was expected to share food and toileting facilities! These heathens had no sense of proper manners or of the ways to show proper respect to someone from my bloodline. On top of this they had a big hairy, huge smelly thing called a dog! It was like a garbage truck with four legs eating anything that hit the floor before even inspecting it. How could this have ever happened to someone as wonderful as me? I know that this letter is certain to be disturbing to you. However, I am sorry to say that things only went downhill from there.

One year later I was once again transferred along with the crazies to a new place called Indiana. There we were joined by even more crazies and another dog! I was now forced to survive in a confined space with seven crazies, three mixed race felines, and two hairy, smelly, downright disgusting dogs! I had to fight for my share of the food and sneak onto the tables and counters to steal the chicken breasts and pork chops I deserve. Then I got a plan.

I decided to befriend and enlist the help of the other felines to drive this scourge from my life! Make their life miserable! Do whatever it takes to drive them all away. We combined efforts. We started throwing up in shoes, leaving dead mice on pillows, coughing up hairballs on blankets and the one black cat even developed a special trick I like to call the exploding sneeze! These half breeds weren't so bad after all! The big, fat one started running up and down the halls late at night sounding like a heard of elephants and I even personally developed a good strong case of irritable bowel syndrome that really drove the crazies up the wall. Heck I became so good at it that I could even shit and walk at the same time!

I am here to tell you that it has worked! We are now down to zero dogs and just one crazy human left in the house! One by one we felines have made their lives so miserable that they have ran away. Now, phase two is to figure out how to get back to that plane and go back home. I have destroyed this evil sect of lunacy and now am ready to take my place among the feline kings. They will all know my name! I can hear it now! They will all be chanting FuzzButt the Great! FuzzButt the Great!

Tale of Four Fairs

I have been to four fairs so far this summer. Who doesn't love a good fair? Well, if you say that you don't then you are certainly missing out on a good time. The key is to be observant of your surroundings. It is possible you may see things you will never ever forget even with therapy. Where oh where do I even begin? I guess let's just start at the first fair I attended. Seems like as good of a place as any.

At fair number one, the funnel cake was decent, better than average I would say. Why do I start off with funnel cake? Well, I feel that you should try to begin with important facts and funnel cake quality is the number one determining factor in fair quality and not one of these red velvet strawberry topped caramel drizzled ones either. The true test is a plain one lightly dusted with powdered sugar. So this fair gets 3.5 stars out of five as an opening score. However, the other memorable moment from this particular fair is what may force me into electroshock treatments. There was a family. A mom, a dad, a son and a daughter. The son had long curly blonde hair. He was all full of energy and excited as you would expect on fair night. The daughter, a tween, was having fun and laughing attempting to ride a mechanical bull without much success. The father was typical fairgoer in jeans and a plaid button down shirt. The mother, oh the mother! There she was, a rather large woman, although in this case I do not know that it would have mattered. But, here she is easily over 200lbs and in blue jean shorts cut so high that a significant portion of her butt cheeks were hanging out the bottom. Just ruined the taste of my funnel cake. Maybe she thought it was sexy. Maybe she needed to think again. That 3.5 star funnel cake just went down to a 1. It all of the sudden just felt more chewy.

On to fair number two. This was a visit to the country fair of my youth. The funnel cake was just a mere 2.5. It was a fun time however. This fair has a parade where the kids collected more candy than on a good Halloween. There also was a real family feel to the place. Being in a small village, most people know one another. It was true Americana. As I said, this was a fair from my youth. My favorite moment from this event was spotting someone I recognized who happened to be a Facebook friend. I hadn't physically seen this person in thirty plus years. But what I did, rather than go up and introduce myself, I took their picture and sent it to them via Facebook message. I then watched them from a distance and they squirmed and turned trying to spot me in the crowd. That was so much fun. Therefore, I will raise this funnel cake experience to a final score of 3.5.

Fair number three was a smallish affair for the size of the town, but it had its own merits. The funnel cake was a 3.0 except for the fact that they also offered a mega funnel cake! It was the size of a medium pan pizza! Even for an enthusiast like me, that was too much. Boy that one would have been perfect for the days when I still had a houseful of kids! Kudos to the funnel cake man for that idea! This fair did have a very cool t-shirt vendor that made old fashioned funny t-shirts on the spot for $10 and I did enter for a chance to win a four wheeler in a drawing in September. I am looking forward to that because I know my chances are probably only like one in 50,000 or so.

Number four was the State Fair. Elizabeth called up and said that she and Douglas wanted Will and I to go with them. We were going to go catch the fair train and ride it into town. This fair has an old passenger train that is only used for special events, weddings, parties, school trips and the State Fair. What is nice is that it eliminates parking and traffic hassles and gives you a ride right to the front gates. This is by far the largest of the fairs I have attended this year. Probably larger than the other three combined. You could probably house some entire fairs just inside the swine barn at this event. This one is a big deal for farmers. Bragging rights of being state champion must be impressive. I saw cows getting washed and blow dried and fluffed up for competition. I wouldn't be surprised if a few of those bulls were using Brylcreem. Anyhow, the funnel cake here was a 4.0. There were actually several vendors with them, but I scanned and scoped and selected what looked to be the best one. I got a golden brown cake with a light dusting of sugar and enjoyed. The rows of food vendors in general seemed endless at this fair. I got some freshly made pork rinds and chocolate ice cream with a peanut butter ribbon in it. Douglas had a burger and steak and onions … actually, it seemed like Douglas was eating the whole five hours that we were there. I kinda lost track of what he had. Elizabeth and Will each had a chocolate covered cheesecake on a stick and Will even had the deep fried Mac-N-Cheese. I saw one man about 6'2, 250lbs wearing a t-shirt that said " I Beat Anorexia" Douglas said it looked more like he had decimated it! I was quite impressed with the guy who used a Dewalt drill to make curly fries. He had some sort of special bit for it. He could do a whole tater in about five seconds. This place had several rides that if you ate too much would help you to fix that problem. One was kinda like a Ferris Wheel with only two spindles sticking out. It was very high like a big Ferris Wheel and it spun so fast that your chair would sometimes flip upside down and clear over. I didn't dare stand under it for fear that someone's partially digested corndog might come flying out. The state lottery had a big setup at the fair . They even had special $1 scratch off tickets that were just for the fair. These tickets, along with cash prizes also had the chance to win a prize wheel spin for various lottery merchandise … t-shirts, hats mugs, stuff like that. I got brave and bought five tickets. I won! I won a cowbell! So exciting! I also won a padded lunch tote! Life changing, I tell ya! Oh, and I won $100. How's that for luck? Went to the fair and made money! Overall this funnel cake got a 4.9 because it gave me a good 6 or 7 hours with my family and a C note in my pocket!

Racquetball Man

I love to play racquetball. It is such a fast paced and challenging game. Just in case you are unfamiliar with the sport, let me try to explain it in layman's terms. You build a room forty feet long by twenty feet wide and twenty feet high. You install a finished hardwood floor and walls capable of withstanding the impact of balls, racquets and 250 pound humans running at full speed and sometimes headfirst. Next, you paint a few lines on the floor to show the service area and then you insert two to four people in the room and play tennis with a very bouncy ball. The ball is so bouncy that is has been clocked at over 190 miles per hour during a game. Now, are you with me so far? Good! Now, every time a player hits the ball it must hit the front wall before it hit's the floor. It is permitted to hit any other wall or the ceiling either before or after the front wall, but it just cannot hit the floor. Now, AFTER it hits the front wall, it can hit any other walls or the ceiling and is permitted to bounce once and only once on the floor before the opponent must hit the ball again to the front wall before hitting the floor! Got it? Okay, I will wait a minute while you catch up. Okay ready? Well, maybe it will make more sense in a minute. You score points by getting your opponent to miss hitting the front wall before the ball hits the floor and only when you have served the ball. If your opponent served the ball and you made him or her miss, then you get to serve. So all you have to do is lock two to four adults in a room and basically play tennis as described above at 190mph.

I play with a variety of people. In the past year it has looked like a United Nations convention. I have played an Afghan, Iranian, Iraqi, Korean, a Filipino-Italian (how the heck did that happen), and a few typical Hoosiers both white and African American … oh and don't forget the big Italian from Brooklyn. He left the match with partially torn knee ligaments. Yep! I worked him over good! The matches are highly competitive and lots of fun. Of course, with everyone locked inside a room vying for the same space, things can get ugly. Just in the past year, I have torn a calf muscle, strained my Achilles tendon, suffered a deep boob bruise and had a freely bleeding cut right between the eyes caused by a racquet. It was my own racquet, but that's beside the point. I was trying to hit the ball as it bounced off the back wall. My racquet hit the wall instead of the ball and then bounced up and hit me between the eyes. I now have a permanent dent there, but I am still a handsome devil so it's ok.

The worst accident of the past year came from playing with Wendy. She was anxious to get out there and play with all 120 pounds of her bad self! We were playing right along when she hit a ball that made me run forward towards the front wall at full speed ahead. Somehow Wendy got between me and the ball and I suddenly looked like Brian Urlacher planting a quarterback on Sunday afternoon. It was ugly! Maybe that's why she decided I wasn't the right guy for her. I am surprised she didn't lose a few teeth!

The reason I am writing today about racquetball is that I am getting ready to go for an elbow MRI. Something has gone awry in there and it hurts when I play. Something akin to tennis elbow I assume. The pain radiates down to the back of my hand when I straighten my arm. Will it stop me? No! I am an addict! I love the danger of being in a room where faceplants into a solid wall are the norm. That's right! I am a mean tough fifty-one year old fat guy! GRRRRRR!!!

Wendy

Wendy appeared in my life as a new coworker one Fall or two ago. She was an attractive, professional looking woman. Smartly dressed. Vibrant, bubbly personality. She seemed like a good fit for the office. She was a few years older than me, but full of energy. I noticed her good qualities.

After a few months had passed, I had occasion to have lunch with Wendy to discuss business. I wanted to ask her to help with some of the people I was training. I felt that she could be a good example for them. During these lunches, I noticed something more. I noticed that she and I did lots of laughing and seemed to enjoy the time spent together.

As luck would have it, not long after those lunch meetings, I fell into a couple of last minute tickets to an NBA game in town. Of course me being the nice guy that I am and Wendy being new to town, I decided to ask her if she would like to go with me, as friends of course.

Actually, she wasn't really new to the area, but she had moved back to the area after being gone for most of her adult life. She had been in Florida and then in Maine for several years before deciding to return to Indiana to be closer to her family, who lived about ninety minutes north of me. It turns out, she was staying with her family and commuting the ninety minutes to the office until she could get settled in and find a place of her own. I guess I should have known that anyone that moves from Florida to Maine must have some issues! Who the heck does that?

Okay, back to my story ... Wendy actually said yes to going to the game with me. She later said that she had even surprised herself by agreeing to go. I am not sure what she meant by that. She probably thought I was out of her league or something. She was probably afraid she wouldn't be able to control herself around me. Yes, I bet that's it!

We had a great time. The conversation flowed. We enjoyed the company. It was a great outing between two people becoming friends. But she was darned cute. She was smart. She was energetic. She was classy. But we worked in the same office! But, she was clear on the other side and I wasn't her boss and she was darned cute. Office romances are trouble and can create tension. But, we are both old enough to handle those sorts of things and dang is she cute!

Days passed. We had phone conversations. We met for lunch. We met for dinner. We somehow got into discussing the possibility of dating. But we both had to be adult about the possibility of what could happen if things did not work out. We worked in the same office. But, darn she was cute! After some discussion, to be on the safe side, Wendy and I decided that I should talk to my bosses about this. I agreed. I went to my boss and told her. She was all for it. She then called in her boss so I could share this potential situation with him, just to have all of my bases covered. His name was Remo.

Remo was the grand old man for the company in Indiana. He was an active 72 yr old man with 38 years of experience. He walks in, sits down, my boss said "Lynn has something important to tell you."

I looked at Remo and said, "I would like to get your blessing before I do something. There is someone here in the office that I would like to date."

Remo interrupted me, "Stop right there! You don't have to say another word. I knew before you knew! And it's ok. I am fine with that."

"But how could you know?" I asked.

"Oh it's easy! When you have been around as long as I have you can just tell. I could tell by the way she acted when you were around her." he smiled.

And that was that, Wendy and I were a dating couple. We did decide to keep it a secret around the office for awhile though. The coming out night was a few weeks later. My boss called me up and said, " I have tickets to the corporate suite tonight, but you can only come if you bring Wendy." She felt it was time to let the world in on our secret. So, away we went! We arrived together and sat together. Yet, to some it was still not adding up. One co-worker actually went up to my boss and said, "We ought to get those two together. They would make a cute couple!"

"Uh, I think they have already taken care of that!" my boss replied.

As it turns out, everyone was quite supportive and the world was good.

Wendy and I shared a great summer. I met her family. She met mine. We worked together, played together. We did so much together. It was a very positive experience. It was comfortable. Concerts and plays. Cookouts and dinners. We were sharing life and enjoying it.

One day Wendy asked me to come sit down. She said she had something she needed to discuss with me.

"I don't want to do this anymore." she said. "We are just two very different people from different backgrounds. You are a great guy, but not MY great guy."

Just like that it was over. It wasn't someone else. It wasn't a big fight. It was just over.

Life is like that. People come and go for all sorts of reasons. Cherish each of them while they are here. You never know when they may just disappear.

Ham Salad

I ran into the store to pick up some milk and ham salad. Honestly, it was my second store I had entered. The much larger mega grocery did not have a lick of ham salad in the place. All they had was that crap called "sandwich spread". They try to pass it off as ham salad, but you ain't fooling me! It just isn't nearly as good in my always perfect opinion. So, I went to the smaller "neighborhood" type store and found the real deal. I got my tub of ham salad and my organic milk. Why organic? First of all it tastes much better. I can't tell you why but it does. Second, just look at the expiration date. The one I bought doesn't expire for another seven weeks! Why the difference between this and the regular stuff? I don't know. Could you Google that for me and let me know what you find out?

So, I have my milk and my ham salad. I get up neat the checkout and was shocked! They have out Kandy Korn and Halloween packages of the good stuff! All sorts of Halloween sweets on display! Um, Mister Store Manager, Halloween is a full THREE MONTHS AWAY!!! Those poor kids will be eating stale treats! Now, I realize Mister Store Manager that Halloween, being my birthday and all, is a very big deal. But, I don't think that stale Kandy Korn is going to do much to preserve the wholesome image of my own personal holiday. Might I suggest you order a fresh batch about the first of October and take this stuff you have on the shelf and send it back to the stupid buyer for your company who thought this was a good idea. Thank you for your time, Mister Store Manager. You have a pleasant day now!

There ! One major disaster averted!

Now, I have my milk and my ham salad. I am driving home along a scenic street that is a well-traveled thoroughfare in a line of traffic. As I turned onto a street that leads into my neighborhood, I found myself following another car. We both were driving slowly up the street. Suddenly, she stopped right in the middle of the street, jumped out of her car, ran over to a nearby yard, bent over and threw up. She then runs back to her car, jumps in, and proceeds merrily on her way down the street. What the heck was that all about? I can understand feeling ill. Could she just not find a plastic bag? How about she just open the car door and hurl onto the street? Did she happen to know the guy that lives there? Did she not like him or something? What will he think if he goes out there to mow? Or worse, I wonder if he has a dog. You know if he lets that dog out to pee it will run straight to that pile of puke and ... well, you know. Then, the dog will run back inside and lick his master's face. Talk about doggie breath!

So, anyhow, I drive the final block to my house, get out of the car and go inside carrying my milk and my, my, oh my that ham salad sure looks a lot like ... That damned woman just ruined my whole trip!

Leading the Cheers

Wendy forced me to do it! I didn't have a choice! What was I to do? I had to go! Sadie was in the competition! Who is Sadie? Oh, that is Wendy's niece. Wendy wanted to go and she had two tickets. What was I going to say? I am too nice of a guy to say no to going with her to watch Sadie compete in the finals competition to select the Indianapolis Colts cheerleaders for the new season! Yay! ... er I mean it's just a bunch of young, beautiful women in swimsuits and cheerleader outfits strutting their stuff and dancing! Yippee! ... er ... I mean ... I think I can survive a couple of hours of that. They are even having the Lombardi Trophy there. I will get to touch the trophy! That's why I am going.

Sadie has already been a Colts cheerleader for a couple of years. She is also a college student. Did you know that they don't even pay those girls? Sadie is not what you would expect of a cheerleader in her personal life. When we go to her parent's house for dinners and such, she is so soft spoken and quiet. She is a lovely girl, but what I would consider conservative. Yet she is one of the ones on TV on Sundays. It is tough to see her as the same girl.

So, anyhow, I slaved my way through the entire evening of watching over fifty gorgeous girls do their dances and performances on stage. I somehow made it through (without rushing the stage even once). Of course I was sitting next to a very gorgeous girl in her own right. Wendy is no slacker in the looks department (hopefully that line will keep her from hurting me when she reads this). It was actually kinda fun to see if my picks matched the judges. In some cases, they were spot on, in other cases the judges got it all wrong. Like why did they pick that one girl with the big teeth? She is cute but those fangs are going to scare some spectators. Maybe she is to be performing on the visitors side of the field.

I think here were a couple of the girls that kept staring at me while they performed. I hope my charming looks were not a distraction. I swear one even did the call me sign while she was dancing. Fortunately Wendy was looking the other way at that moment. I was probably the number one topic of backstage gossip.

Sadie? Well, she didn't make the cut this year. It is a tough competition and she did make it through for two years so she has no reason to feel too bad. I am just happy that she decided to try out again so that I could go and spend two hours sitting beside the prettiest girl in the whole place (there, that ought to score me some big points at home)!

Carly

Carly is an inspiration to me. We met a couple of years ago professionally and we hit it off right away. She is a sweet soul with a kind, soft personality. She cares about others and sometimes that is what gets her into trouble. She is too giving. That's a good fault to have.

Carly is one of these people that everyone hates because even though she is in her forties, she looks about sixteen. She has children who look older than her! Her kids range from their early twenties down to probably elementary school age. She has probably five or so boys. She has been married to the same man all these years.

One of the things that impressed me about Carly is that she is currently such a little thing. I don't know women's sizes very well, but without asking, I would guess her to be a size six. Now you realize that if she is a size four that she will probably physically harm me for assuming she is fatter than she is. But trust me, she is skinny, healthy skinny. Carly at one point in her life was a size twenty-two. No, that is not a misprint. She was a whopper! But through hard work and determination, she transformed herself. I have to say that I greatly admire her strength.

Over time Carly and I became quite good friends. We just had a connection in a way that we could confide in one another. Sometimes you just develop that with certain people for inexplicable reasons. We laughed together and cried together over life's trials and tribulations. It was good for both of us.

Earlier this year, I found out that Carly had a secret. A secret that she hadn't even shared with me. For twenty plus years, Carly has been a battered wife. It had finally reached a boiling point where she simply could not take it anymore. She had finally grown as a person to where she knew that she deserved better. Was it a difficult time? Yes. Did she face uncertainty and struggles? Yes. Was it worth it? Yes. She is now blossoming and her soon to be ex-spouse has even stepped up to the plate as a responsible father in this time of greatest need for their children. It is turning into a happy ending. A perfect ending? No. But a good result.

Did I tell you how much I admire this strong woman? Carly and I have a special little bond. One of my favorite moments occurred shortly after the separation from her husband. Carly was at her sister's house talking to me on the phone. As the call ended, I said what I always say to Carly and she responded as she always does with "I love you too, Lynn!" As Carly hung up the phone, her sister bounced around the corner wondering who the heck Lynn was and why Carly was telling them she loved them! Carly then explained that there was nothing to fear. This was just the way we have always ended our conversations. And you know what? For me, it feels wonderful every time!

Graham Cracker Caper

I have a problem. I bought some graham crackers at the store the other day because I have been craving graham crackers and milk. See, I have been eating lots of fruits and vegetables for my health but it is ok to treat yourself every once in a while. So the other day I made sure to get milk and grahams. Not much better than dunking and eating those. A little while ago I decided that tonight was the night. It was time to enjoy my special treat. I sauntered out to the kitchen. Of course FuzzButt was there. He is always right there. He has superb hearing and will take off at the speed of light through the dining room so that he is right there waiting by his food bowl when you arrive. The wet food bowl. He can have dry and treats and water, but that canned food one stays empty. If you put out too much he will still hog it all down and then go throw it up in my shoe or on my pillow, but he will not leave a speck for anybody else.

I did have fun watching FuzzButt and Smokey tonight. Around dusk there were two big rabbits playing in my backyard. Smokey spotted them first and of course FuzzButt had to see what was going on. They watched those rabbits play for a good fifteen minutes. I heard them talking about "if only they could get outside" Shoot, those rabbits were bigger and faster than my two lazy cats, but they still thought they could catch them if given a chance.

But, back to my problem. I went to the kitchen for my treat. I opened the cabinet under the counter. Not there. Hmmm … Maybe I put them over where I put dry goods. Nope. Well then they have to be in the spice cabinet. No again! Then it caught my eye. There was an empty graham cracker box in the kitchen trash can! My whole box gone! There is currently only one other occupant in this house and that is Will. He must be the guilty party. Now, I did not specifically tell him to not eat my grahams, but I sure as hell am going to hide them better next time!

The Roast

I am here to tell you that my mommy thought I was nuts! She thought I didn't have "a lick of sense".

Well, I am here to tell you that I showed her! Sometimes for Sunday dinners when I was growing up, she would prepare a beef roast for dinner. It was a big deal. She would thaw the roast beginning the day before. She would then get up and put the roast in the skillet and brown it on Sunday morning before sticking it into the oven. It would remain there the better part of the day. About one hour before dinner, she would take out the roast and add carrots and potatoes and onions. She said this was so they wouldn't just all go to mush. An hour later, dinner was served. Dinner was good. The daylong process was complete.

One day I told my mommy that she has been going about it all wrong all of these years. I told her about how I take a frozen roast and throw it in the pan, add water, carrots, potatoes, onions and a packet of dry brown gravy mix to sprinkle on the top. I then pop the whole thing in the oven about 10:00, pull it out at 4:00 and eat it!

Her response? "Oh God!" She thought I had a screw loose! "The meat would be tough and the vegetables cooked down to nothing!" she said, "That couldn't possibly be good!"

As fate would have it, not too many weeks after that conversation, she found herself in a predicament. Someone in the community had a death in the family. In her rural community, when someone dies, everyone brings food to the family. It is just a tradition. When mom learned of this event, there wasn't much time to act. She decided that she wanted to make one of those good beef roasts she had in the freezer. The trouble was that by the time she had figured all of this out, there was no time for thawing and browning and such. So, she threw caution to the wind and tried it MY way! She told me that she had been very concerned about her reputation as a cook in the community as she delivered this "cheaters roast" to the poor grieving family. She just kept her fingers crossed that it simply wasn't too horrible.

About a week later the family delivered my mom back her roasting pan. The lady also told mom that several people wanted to know her recipe for making a roast as it was the best they had ever had! Uh huh! That's right! MY roasting tip had made her a celebrity in the community! Needless to say, my mom makes her roasts my way now!

Jury Duty

I received a postcard in the mail today. It said Summons for Jury. You are ordered to call us within the next fourteen days to qualify for jury service. Failure to do so could result in a finding of contempt of court! It is an honor to serve as a juror. Other than the phone number, that was it. Short and sweet. But wait a minute! I have a real problem with this! I could be found in contempt of court if the mailman delivered this postcard to the wrong address and it got trashed? Well, that hardly seems fair! Also, this card gives me fourteen days. What if I was on a three week trip to Aruba? Would they throw me in the slammer when I got home? I am much too pretty to go to jail! Oh, and it does also say to bring this card when I report for service and that I am a prospective juror for the week of September 15th. Like I can really keep track of this card until then. They must be dreaming.

I was summoned to jury duty in Tennessee one time. You had to call each night to see if you needed to report the next day. Then a couple days I had to go in and sit around and wait. The second day there were a couple of lawyers asking me questions. I think they thought I might be a keeper. I tried to seal the deal by telling them about how I had been abducted by an alien species and implanted with a photographic memory chip and a lie detector chip that beeps every time someone is untruthful. That one must have been malfunctioning that day because it was beeping like crazy every time that one lawyer fellow opened his mouth. I don't know why, but they did not choose me to be a juror. I was disappointed. They were paying like $15.00/ day to be there. They did have the nice court officer to show me how to get out of that place. He walked me all the way to the front doors.

Actually, I should probably behave myself this time and keep quiet. They seem to like the quiet ones. I bet I could get some good stories for my next book out of the experience. I could even be the holdout juror that is the only one to have reasonable doubt so that they have to put us up in a swanky hotel for a few nights while we ponder the fate of a purse snatcher. I have a little time here so I need to get busy putting together a game plan. I will be sure to let you know if I am going to be on Court TV. Wait a minute! I bet that is it! There is some high profile case coming up and they need photogenic jurors like me for the TV production! I am so smart!

Animal Masters

I write a good bit these days about the cats. That is because at the moment I am servant to four of them. I have nothing against dogs or other critters, but it is just the way things have turned out. I was actually down to just two. Elizabeth and Douglas had taken FuzzButt and Smoky for a while. But, then there were these two puppies found in an abandoned warehouse and Elizabeth just had to bring them home. She asked me if FuzzButt and Smoky could come over to my house temporarily until she and Douglas found a home for the puppies. Well, they found them a home alright! They even had a privacy fence built in the backyard a couple weeks ago. I don't think FuzzButt and Smoky are leaving anytime soon. I have plenty of room here. It's just me and Will and we have seven bedrooms and Will is only here during college breaks. I just do not need this many critters to care for.

They do provide entertainment. I recall the time the lady called to confirm an appointment for one of the older cats to be spayed. I answered the phone and she said, "Mr. Hewitt. I was just calling to confirm that we were going to get Lucky tomorrow!" I wasn't quite sure how to answer and stood there silently for a moment. The lady then realized the proposition she had just made and babbled her way through the rest of the call.

FuzzButt has this little 2 inch square cloth sack filled with catnip. I bought it at a craft show many months ago. He has it a filthy mess because he carries it with him almost everywhere. He will throw it down and then pounce on it and beat it up for trying to escape. He will then pick it back up and continue on his merry way.

Smoky is FuzzButt's best buddy. The children think these two must be gay because they are always together and rarely interact at all with the two female cats in the house. Smoky is just mister laid back cool as a cucumber. That is until he sees a shadow on the wall. Then, he goes wall jumping and swatting trying to catch that shadow. He never seems to grow tired of that game.

Lastly is the oldest of the bunch. Goldie is sixteen and as active as ever. She loves when you chase her down the hall. She will duck under the bed in my room and wait for me to enter. Then, she will take off in the other direction toward the kitchen where she will sit and have an asthma attack while waiting on me to come get her some turkey from the fridge.

I would love to have a dog, but right now I am overwhelmed by all of these cats. We had a great dog for many years and she passed away of old age about three years ago. Wendy had an old dog that was around the house here a good bit last summer. It was a retriever and was very little trouble. But in between those was a guy named Duke.

Duke was a mix of Beagle and Jack Russell Terrier. He needed a home and I gave him one. The trouble was I am not so sure he wanted my home. This old guy who had no place to keep him gave him to me. The trouble was when you take the nose of a Beagle and put it on a hyper Jack Russell Terrier, the damned thing will follow that nose anywhere! I lost that dog more in a few months than I have lost my car keys in a lifetime. Once he caught a scent, he lost his brain. He was quite sociable. I would find him in various peoples yards playing with kids or just hanging out. He just lacked common sense. He didn't seem to know to come back home, or else he just didn't want to. Finally one day we were outside working in the yard and he disappeared and we never saw him again. We did look. We also did check with the pound and so on. One day a couple months later, I did see a dog on a leash on a walk with a woman, but I didn't dare go investigate for fear she might want to give him back!

Back to the Books

Today is college movein day for Will. This is the beginning of his sophomore year. This is my eighth move-in day in eight years, so I am an old pro at this. It all started with my stepson Jared and then made its way through Shelly and Elizabeth and now Will. This may actually be my last one although you never know. The reason I say that is that the others at some point decided to just get an apartment and stop moving back and forth. I don't know what Will may decide to do.

He began preparing for this move a few days ago. He did so by loading my kitchen sink up with a pile of dirty dishes from his room and hauling out a garbage bag full of trash from in there. He also filled the laundry room with piles of dirty clothes. I had seen this all before many times so I was prepared. College kids think that by making these placements, that every thing will just magically happen and by the day they leave, all of the clothes will be washed and folded for them just to put them in a tote and haul them off. I made sure not to shatter Will's fantasy world just yet.

The next stage began late yesterday. I call it the living room staging. Will began to pile most of his belongings in the middle of the living room floor so that they would be readily handy to load into the two cars this morning. Yes, one kid, one shared dorm room, two carloads of stuff. Of course there were clothes and bedding and a fan and video games. Those are all fairly typical. But two items in his pile caught my attention. One is a black and white stuffed rabbit named Sugarloaf. Will first got the rabbit when he was quite young and he asked what its name was. His sister looked at the manufacturer's tag on it and it said Sugarloaf. I guess that is the name of the company that made it, but needless to say, the name stuck and Will, at nineteen, still takes Sugarloaf with him to college. The other item that caught my eye was his banjo-mandolin. Will does not play any musical instruments, but this one was given to him by his grandfather when he was just a little tike. He guards it with his life and seems quite attached to it. That makes me proud that he cares about something like that.

Will's scheduled move-in time was set for 1:00pm. This actually meant that he had to get up a little earlier than normal so that we could leave the house by noon-ish. When we first arrived, we were walking up a sidewalk heading to a check-in station when this very attractive young woman caught my eye from a distance. She had her arms thrown up in the air with a big smile on her face and she was running full tilt in my direction. I immediately felt sorry for Will that his celebrity book author father had been recognized. I really wanted this to be his day. The beautiful girl ran across the street and right past me! To Will! She was all excited and gave him big hugs! But wait, am I not supposed to be the one getting hugged by good looking fans? She is probably just using him to get an autographed copy of my next book when it comes out.

I do not feel sorry for Will this year. He knows the lay of the college landscape. He has tons of friends. His dorm looks like a four star hotel. The elevator actually stops on every floor. The place is air conditioned. He is also only steps away from a huge cafeteria offering just about every cuisine known to man. The poor guy has it so tough. It is so bad that I am thinking about going back to college myself. I even stopped by a couple a sorority houses today and offered my services as a House Mother. I think I would be ideal for the position.

www.ingramcontent.com/pod-product-compliance
Lightning Source LLC
Chambersburg PA
CBHW031958040426
42448CB00006B/405